Home Again

Stories of migration and return

Home Again
Stories of migration and return

Compiled by CELIA SORHAINDO
and POLLY PATTULLO

for the Dominica UK Association

PAPILLOTE PRESS
London and Roseau, Dominica

First published in Great Britain in 2009

A CIP catalogue record for this book is available from the British Library.

Typeset in Novarese

Printed by Imprint in India
Design by Andy Dark

ISBN: 978-0-9532224-5-2

Papillote Press
23 Rozel Road
London SW4 0EY
United Kingdom
www.papillotepress.co.uk
and Trafalgar, Dominica

NOTES

The publisher would like to thank the participants for the loan of their personal photographs. All contemporary photographs are by Celia Sorhaindo.

Currency is shown in €C$, US$ and pound sterling. Exchange rates at time of going to press were: US$1 = €C$2.7 £1=€C$3.9

Celia Sorhaindo was born in Dominica and moved to the UK at the age of eight. She returned to Dominica in 2005.

Polly Pattullo is a journalist and the publisher of this book.

Contents

Foreword

The idea of a book focusing on returnees to Dominica originated at the general meeting of the Dominica UK Association (DUKA) held in London in September 2007. Under the "reports and information exchange" item of the agenda, DUKA's past vice-chair and local representative in Dominica Franklyn Georges reported on his experiences following his recent re-settlement on the "Nature Island". While enjoying Dominica's beauty and tranquillity, some returnees, he said, appeared to experience a degree of isolation as they sought to re-adjust. This feeling was more pronounced among residents returning from the UK who were sometimes referred to as "English" in marked contrast to ex-US compatriots who were viewed as Dominican. This may be explained by the more recent emigration experience of the latter group, but it nevertheless remains a sensitive issue. The situation could not be treated as trivial as it reflected deeper concerns that needed to be addressed such as the anecdotal claims that returnees to Dominica are only valued for their money. DUKA members agreed that the experiences of returnees warranted some positive response through an investigation and exposure of their experiences to a wider public. So the foundations for a publication were truly laid.

The purpose of this book then is to catalogue the journeys and experiences of individual Dominican returnees and thereby break the "wall of silence" that all too frequently encourages suspicion and prejudice. It also aims to address the myth that life experiences in "Motherland" England or, indeed, elsewhere were either a "bed of roses" or riddled with constant challenges.

As a way of sharing these different journeys, I hope that Home

Again will both entertain the reader and foster an appreciation of some of those who emigrated – mainly for economic reasons – from the mid-1950s onwards to the UK, and later to the US, Canada and elsewhere, but who have returned to live and work in Dominica. A minority of the stories, of those born in other countries but who are now "Home Again" to their "Nature Island", provides a special twist and points to a door of opportunity for those still resident overseas.

The personal histories depicted in Home Again contribute to the focus on togetherness that underpinned the strap-line for Reunion 2008: "Celebrating the Journey Together". I hope the stories will help to resolve any misconceptions – the perceived wealth of returnees or an inadvertent display of grandeur – for it is humility that best characterises the lives of these journeying men and women. The cross-cutting themes that permeate their experiences are particularly significant and useful to those interested in the social history of migration. The book also highlights the networking and support dimensions of the overseas Dominican associations, and the sustained personal commitment of those who hope to realise their dreams.

Home Again succeeds both in fostering a better understanding while also giving deserved recognition to those Dominicans who have made important contributions both to their host countries and to their homeland over the last half century, and who continue to do so – now from their home base.

It is hoped that you will find the book interesting, informative and a source of encouragement in whatever you do.

Vincent M John, chairman, Dominica UK Association (DUKA)
& Mas Domnik UK

Dominica

The map shows the main places mentioned in this book and parish boundaries. Dominica is situated in the eastern Caribbean between the islands of Guadeloupe and Martinique. Approximately 47km long and 26km wide, it is wild and mountainous with many rivers and waterfalls; much of the island is covered in rainforest.

Introduction

Global migration has influenced the shape of the modern world and in many countries immigration has become a topical and controversial subject. But rarely is the focus on those migrants who make the journey back to the place they regard as home. Home Again is a selection of interviews with 22 people who left the eastern Caribbean island of Dominica to live overseas and then to return, sometimes after 40 years or more. Each account documents their early days in Dominica, life in a new country, the decision to return and, most importantly, the experience of being back home. A former British colony, Dominica has been an independent nation since 1978.

Documenting the life stories of these Dominicans is important and timely. We are at a unique point in history when those who left in the 1950s and 1960s during a period of mass migration are reaching retirement age and many are coming home, mainly from the UK. The book also includes another group who are rarely mentioned – a younger generation of returnees, including those of Dominican parentage who were born overseas.

Of the 22 men and women featured in Home Again, 17 settled in the United Kingdom, three in the United States, one in Canada and one in Barbados. They left Dominica between 1957 and 1975 and range in age from 40 to 73 years. They came from all sorts of backgrounds and worked as nurses, trade union officials, London transport drivers, social workers, care workers, teachers, clerks, chefs, and in factories. Among our 22 Dominicans there is also a software engineer, a scientist, a scuba diving instructor, a mannequin maker for Madame Tussauds, and a mayor of a London borough. Two returnees moved back to Dominica two decades ago, but most have returned within the last five years.

Most stayed away for decades – although they had planned to be away for only five years. Indeed, the desire to return began from the day they left Dominican shores. Dominican novelist Phyllis Shand Allfrey claimed "love for an island is the sternest passion" and this sentiment echoes across the stories. They may have left Dominica but Dominica never left them. In telling their stories, they make an important contribution to Dominica's history.

The pattern of coming and going is central to Dominica. Its first inhabitants were Amerindians from the Orinoco basin in South America. Later, Europeans arrived as the French and British laid claim to Dominica. In the eighteenth century, slaves were brought from West Africa. Today, the majority of Dominica's population are descendants of these early arrivals.

But Dominica has been shaped as much by those who have left as those who arrive. In common with other Caribbean countries, Dominica has a long history of economic migration – starting with departures for the gold fields of South America in the nineteenth century and later, to Trinidad, Panama, Aruba, Curaçao, the French Caribbean islands, and North America. But after the second world war came a new opportunity. The British 1948 Nationality Act granted all Commonwealth subjects the rights of citizenship in the United Kingdom. At the same time, Britain was suffering from a chronic labour shortage. And in 1948 the SS Empire Windrush set sail from

Jamaica to England with 492 passengers lured by the promise of work. Although no Dominicans were on board, that journey marked the start of events which would change the face of the Caribbean and the UK forever.

The numbers of people leaving the Caribbean as a whole for the UK rose from a trickle in the late 1940s to over 2,000 in 1953, peaking at 70,000 in 1961 just before the 1962 Commonwealth Immigrants Act (this only permitted those with government-issued employment vouchers to settle in the UK). Between 1955 and 1960 a total of 6,296 Dominicans left for the UK of whom nearly two-thirds were men, and 70% were 30 or under. Nearly one third of this total left in 1960. This was migration on a scale never experienced before, to a country culturally and environmentally very different and far enough away to make returning home often financially unfeasible.

Between 1959 and 1962 it is estimated that 14% of Dominica's population of 61,783 migrated to the UK. The ravages of hurricane David in 1979 triggered the start of another exodus from the island, and between 1981 and 1993, one quarter of the population left, this time mainly to US and Canada.

Currently, it is thought that up to 200,000 adult Dominicans live abroad: around 40% are in the US, a similar percentage in other Caribbean countries, and most of the remainder in the UK and Canada. Unfortunately, no statistics are available of those who return.

Many of the interviewees in Home Again recall growing up in Dominica with a great deal of fondness – childhood freedoms, and adventures such as cricket, dominoes, hunting, story-telling, swimming, fishing. But in adulthood, job shortages pushed them to leave at the same time as they were drawn by opportunities overseas. Going away was not a rejection of home, it was perceived as a way to help those left at home. For those going to the UK, the island's colonial relationship with Britain meant that many saw migration to the "mother country" as, symbolically, going home.

However many migrants did not, and still do not, always tell family and friends back home about the realities of life in the new country. These stories include the negative aspects of leaving such as separation, hardship, prejudice and culture shock. Of course, there were also positive features: material benefits, educational opportunities and the chance to interact with other cultures.

Those interviewed for Home Again also told us of how they sent money back for family and friends, and supported community projects, especially during times of crisis such as after Hurricane David. Many also worked with Dominican organisations to raise funds, to maintain connections with the island and its culture, and to socialise. Remittances by Dominicans overseas have been significant and were estimated at EC$176 million in 2007 (about 16% of its GDP).

The important role of family is very evident in these accounts, and in the majority of cases family members helping each other made the transition from one culture to another easier. Those at home funded passages so that other relatives could leave; migrating parents left children with remaining family members until they were able to send for them. Those settled in new countries sent for their relatives, welcomed them on arrival, fed, clothed, housed them and found them employment. And those who remained in Dominica purchased land, managed home builds and provided continuity and the vital connection, for those returning.

Home Again highlights the highs and lows of what it has been like to come home – to be a "returnee". Everyone talked of the wonderful environment, a sense of mental and physical well-being, a re-connection and a feeling of belonging. But there was also discussion of rejection, isolation, and the frustrations generated by a slower pace, and by the lack of facilities, goods and services. Some returnees felt that they are regarded as "cash cows" and are seen as arrogant. They highlighted how they brought back valuable skills and knowledge and different ideas to Dominica, contributed capital and created employment. Some also lamented that those skills and experiences are largely under utilised or ignored.

Dominica has one of the highest rates of migration in the world, with more than 80% of its work force with secondary education migrating. Ensuring that a percentage of those who leave do return are important considerations for the development of the country. A robust local population, which includes educated and enterprising people, is required for economic growth, to maintain family structure, to care for the elderly and to foster culture and national identity.

Home Again highlights the contributions of Dominicans residing overseas and the important role they play in mitigating the negative impact of migration. Furthermore, it highlights the need for all Dominicans, those who remain, those who reside abroad and those who return, to show tolerance, respect and understanding to each other, to establish common goals and work together for the continued development of the country.

My sincere thanks go to Franklyn Georges, Vincent John, the chairman of the Dominica UK Association, and others for the initial concept, support and encouragement throughout the project. To Polly Pattullo for her immense efforts with transcribing, editing and publishing. And a special thank you to all who feature in this book in generously giving of your time, and openly and honestly sharing your stories with us.

Celia Sorhaindo

JEAN POPEAU

Jean Popeau was brought up in Belvedere and left for England in 1957 when he was 11. He became a teacher and gained a PhD in the philosophy and poetry of the Negritude movement. He returned to Dominica in 2008.

J ust before I left Dominica in 1957, the headmaster of my school in Belvedere made me stand up with everyone sitting there, and said: "Who is the one going to England?" And I said, "Me". And he said, "Boy, you're going to be a big shot." I was 11 at the time and the assumption was that one of the reasons you were going to England was to get a better education.

That school, near where I'm now building my home, was basically one large crumbling wooden building – there were no room dividers, just a series of benches and each bench was a class and you had teachers shouting at each class to get your attention. There was a sign that said, "Cleanliness is next to godliness", but there were outside toilets and no facilities for washing your hands. We would get free powdered milk which they would mix every morning to provide something to drink. We learned about England at school, and I probably knew more about English heroes than the fellas I met when I went to school in London. We learned about Rodney and Nelson and their exploits in the Caribbean but not much about the rest of our history. Education was limited to colonial matters.

My father went to England in 1955 to seek some better sort of economic situation. My parents were essentially peasant farmers from La Roche, but it was so dire on the island that it was impossible to get on and look after your family. We would go to our garden which was in the mountains with our mother at the weekend and during school holidays. We would all carry a basket of food and have to cross the White river on foot to get home and if the river was high we would be in trouble. We had to walk everywhere; we only had shoes for going to church, we had few clothes. It was a precarious form of life. Flour and rice and codfish were luxuries but perhaps because all families had poverty in common, as children it didn't hit you hard. The only thing you knew was that children in town were probably better off.

Even so, there was time for enjoyment – dances on a Saturday, cricket matches, celebrations for first communion (photograph previous page), and at Christmas people would celebrate for a whole week; then you would have carnival – and there would be bands going from village to village. There was a great sense of communal activity and caring. Things started to change, however, in the 1950s, when people, especially the men, started going to England. And then you began to get an atmosphere of people saying, "Well if you're getting money from your man and if you want me to do something for you, you'll have to pay for it." Then money started to figure in transactions.

When my father had been in England a couple of years, he decided to send for the rest of us. For my sister and I it seemed that we were going to be plucked away from the island because our father wanted his family with him, and there was no alternative but to adjust to a new way of life. I had mixed feelings about leaving Dominica. On one hand you wanted to get away from the poverty and you were told you would get a better education, on the other hand the natural setting and beauty of the place was still something that struck you. My father would write when he was away but he did not say much – he would write about practical matters like "I have been able to send you a little bit of money, look after it" and so on. We knew that it was cold in England though and that there was prejudice – those stories filtered back. And there was an awareness that there was poverty there because a lot of them were sharing a room, and, wages being limited, they had to really scrimp and save to send any money back home. I didn't have a concept of England as a mother country, but as an alien place that I would have to get used to.

My mother, sister and I left on a Greek ship crowded with emigrants in September 1957. It was an atmosphere of chaos on the ship, children running around and spilling things on people's clothes, belongings spread all over the place. It docked in Genoa and then we went on a train to England where my father met us. We ended up living in the most run-down part of east London you could imagine, among the gasometers of Millwall, on the Isle of Dogs. We lived in a terraced house, in a couple of rooms with my uncle. It was very cramped and crowded. You were basically in very meagre conditions, and you looked out at a dank and rather depressing street. You were suddenly in a very enclosed atmosphere from what you were used to. But then London was still in a state of post-war poverty – terraced houses with no bathrooms and outside toilets, coal fires for heating the rooms.

We had a radio but there was no TV to talk about – and anyway we couldn't afford a television. I enjoyed the radio because it helped me to improve my English – I started to listen avidly and I remember listening to a programme called The Clitheroe Kid – the comedy helped you to get used to the language and the working-class culture. There was also a programme called In Town Tonight about the West End of London, and Vic Oliver's dance music show.

We met people from other Caribbean islands – a lot of men on

> ' They sometimes say to returnees, why don't you go back to England – they see you as complaining too much. But as everyone knows, this island wouldn't be able to continue without those informal contributions that people abroad send back. '

their own, who had left wife and children behind, living in one room as in Samuel Selvon's *Lonely Londoners*. But there were not many children coming from the Caribbean at that time – it was very bleak. People would ignore you when you went to the shops and serve others.

When I arrived there was no time to take the eleven plus exam and there was no real assessment of me so I just fell into an all-white, working-class, secondary modern Catholic school in Poplar. A certain way to ensure that you become an atheist is to go to a Catholic school. It was very run down, there was a lot of disruption, poor behaviour, poor standards. There were the usual racist remarks from the children and also from the teachers, who were really quite ignorant about the Caribbean. I was shocked. The school provided a very crude education and it was assumed that you were factory fodder.

I was a school failure really and came out with only one O Level. But I was interested in science and got a job in a science laboratory doing control work for a factory. I had to educate myself after work with evening classes and part-time study. Eventually, I got qualifications to do a degree, and went to North London Polytechnic as it was then, in 1970, to do a degree in philosophy of all things.

My parents never discussed coming back – it was too early on in that period. But they enjoyed talking amongst themselves about people they knew and funny experiences they'd had back home. There was very little discussion about what was going on in England. Neither of them went back to Dominica. Mother was killed in a car accident in 1966, and father had no interest in going back – which was strange because he didn't really belong in England; he might have enjoyed life better in the Caribbean but he'd cut himself off. By then I was trying to educate myself, and my sister and I were established in England. England was becoming much more a part of your life.

But I'd kept up my interest in the Caribbean. There was something called the Commonwealth Institute in Kensington – with exhibits about Commonwealth countries – and I'd go there and just look at these pictures of the Caribbean, and I'd get into a nostalgic haze about the flora and the fauna. It was basically nostalgia, because I knew there was no work in the Caribbean, and people wanting to emigrate.

My first visit back to Dominica was for about six weeks in 1974. We had a relatively rich aunt who lived in Roseau and I stayed with her, and then with my uncle in La Roche. I was happy – I like fishing and walking, and I went back to that. My needs were not great, but I could see there was a general air of depression. I made inquiries about getting a job in teaching but I couldn't continue my own education here so I decided to go back. It was very vague but I thought at that point that I would want a home here to keep my acquaintance with the island.

I got married in England in 1975 to a Trinidadian, and had two children. I must say I didn't tell them much about Dominica and the kids weren't that interested. We came here as a family in 1992 – my daughter was about 12 and my son was a couple of years older, but they never really took to Dominica, even to visit. I've come to terms with the assumption that my children will identify with British culture – let's face it is a dynamic culture, and there's a new generation of kids who are creating a new culture in which all sorts of inter-cultural interchanges are taking place. It's now a world in which my children can fit. It's a completely different world to the one I emigrated to.

In London, I ran a youth club in Fulham, but didn't like it much so decided to go into teaching. I taught English in secondary schools in east London, then decided to go into multi-cultural education, teaching children who needed a boost to develop their academic work. I also taught privately and met other cultures on a very intimate level. I've taught Muslim children and a Sikh child who was physically handicapped – I had cultural relationships with very different cultures. I also taught in Bedford and then in Dudley, in the Midlands. My best time in England was getting involved in the education system – it expands your horizons in the way that nothing else does.

I stayed in teaching for 30 years – but my primary interest was not in terms of a career but of self-development – I did my Masters degree in the sociology of literature and then for my doctorate I tried to chart the philosophical background of the Negritude movement and the literary way it expressed itself. The movement, led by Aimé Césaire from Martinique and Leopold Senghor from Senegal in the 1930s, was basically a literary attempt to place the black man in the European world of the time and to reject the French policy of assimilation. My thesis was published in 2003 as Dialogues of Negritude by Carolina Academic Press in the States.

My work was, I suppose, my way of coming to terms with my personal relationship with European culture. I felt it helped me to

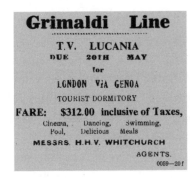

Off to England by sea.
An advertisement in
the Dominica Chronicle
in 1957

root myself in the black world and to try to maintain my contact with this island; I also thought it helped to have some kind of relationship with the black world which is more authentic than just staying in England and losing myself in an English culture. I was constantly aware that I was not born into that culture, and that the first 11 years in that other culture did mark me, and had a profound effect on my thinking about and relationship with European culture.

There are things I'm highly critical of about European culture – its materialism leads to rootlessness, and that affects one's own children; the lack of an authentic relationship with nature and the spiritual drift, and, of course, its attitude to the black world and third world countries in general. And I am heavily critical of certain attitudes of white males – that they see black women as sexual objects – and for that reason I can't get on with some of them. A lot of other things you'd recognise as crudely racist. Therefore that has all shaped the way I see Europe and the way I see my life in Europe.

All this was a reason to maintain contact with a place like this which is rooted in a cultural background with which I am much more sympathetic than the European culture I happened to live in over the years. I felt that my soul never belonged in Europe.

I kept in touch with Dominica through the Chronicle newspaper which I received by post – and, later on, the internet. My sister was also living here – she moved back before I did. At one point, I did join a group who met in Earls Court who were going to do something about the school system in Dominica but I wasn't comfortable there, and then I moved to Bedford. So I really didn't get involved in groups, although I went to DUKA meetings, used to go to their celebrations and I gave a talk for them once.

The actual mental decision about coming back to live started I would say about a decade ago in 1998 when I came on holiday by myself and I made inquiries about getting a piece of land. It starts as a vague wish and then you have to keep questioning yourself and think how am I going to do this. I bought a piece of land in 2002 in Belvedere and I had at the back of my mind that I might build a small place which I can come to as a holiday home. Then in 2004, when my new wife and I visited, we bought an extra piece, and we discussed building about a year or so later. And it took off from there. I came back in January 2008 and started building.

My experiences coming back here have been pretty good. I think I prepared the way: I'm living and working in a place where I am known. I know for other Dominicans who are living in a different community to the one they were brought up in that might be a problem. If you say Ruthina's my sister, then straight away they know you are part of this community. It helps you to fit back in. Then you also need Creole to communicate authentically, especially to the older people. If I came back with a Yankee accent and no Creole, it would have been much more difficult. I learnt Creole as a boy even though they tried to cane it out of you.

When people call you English, it may be on a friendly or an unfriendly basis, because you have an English accent. It may be a way of suggesting you're alien – you're English in your attitude,

‹ I see my return
here as spiritually
uplifting. ›

you're stiff, you're formal, and you don't understand the goings on
here. It's shorthand for saying you don't belong. They seem to
recognise you're English from your walk, your appearance. I've been
called English in town without even opening my mouth. I wonder
how they can work it out. Perhaps you're brisker in your walk, more
purposeful – it could be all sorts of things. But there's an attitude
towards the people who they call the English. In its most benign
form it simply means that you've lived in England for a long time.

What I've experienced is the idea that you're better off. I
remember talking to one guy and I said the pension I'm getting from
England is not that much. He said that it's much higher than a top
civil servant's salary here. It's a widely held view that you're much
better off – and that somehow you should be paying more. You can
afford it, so you ought to be making a bigger contribution. Then the
civil servants think that you hassle more. They will want to deny you
your rights. They sometimes say to returnees, why don't you go back
to England – they see you as complaining too much. But as everyone
knows, this island wouldn't be able to continue without those
informal contributions that people abroad send back.

Migration is a common historical fact within the whole Caribbean
– it's been a very big factor of life. So many of these people have
relatives who have been to other islands to better themselves.
They've all made the attempt. They're all economic migrants. We've
just gone further – it's difficult to understand this resentment for the
people who've gone to England. I got the impression that Yankees
are more admired because US culture is more admired than British

culture. America is somehow seen as a more friendly nation to the Caribbean, whereas England is the colonial culture and so on. The assumption is that you will have picked up some of those embedded colonial attitudes, through osmosis as it were, from having lived in the culture for so long, and you are indirectly bringing them back. I suspect that has a lot to do with it.

The government needs to step in and set a tone. The prime minister needs to set a tone nationally and say we need to recognise that these people have come back, and are making a positive contribution, and we should stop calling them English and say they are Dominicans like the rest of us. If they did that and there was a discussion in the media it would help to change attitudes because so much of this is based, of course, on ignorance.

The situation around returnees creates dynamics which we're obviously experiencing at the moment, and the government would need to get involved more actively if it is to be a successful social development. It just can't be allowed to develop ad hoc without the involvement of the government – it needs a training of the population.

But I see a great complacency here which needs to be tackled if the island is going to progress; there needs to be a certain kind of refusal to accept this complacency. The island won't survive among other Caricom countries unless this complacency, this poor attitude to business and service, is tackled. There needs to be self-criticism – this attitude of "it's our way" and "this is our life style" is ultimately going to cost a hell of a lot. It's much better if this criticism comes from inside – but if it means the returnees doing it, so be it, because we bring some kind of financial clout and, because we're engaged in business, we can make that kind of critical approach. Also there is the question of how does a small state like this survive? At the moment it begs to every Tom, Dick and Harry. That's a big worry for people returning. How can Dominica maintain services, infrastructure, with very few means to produce the finance to service those needs? The survival of the island is a big question mark.

For myself, my wife and I are thinking about opening a book shop, selling books for light reading, and some artefacts, fabric and so on. We would hope to contribute books to the schools and try to develop writing in the island. I am thinking of doing some writing myself based on my experiences here because my whole life has been charted through my writing and what has happened through my educational development. I've done three stories for children based on my childhood here – it was a contribution to a book of short stories, based on ghost themes, called Under the Storyteller's Spell. So I will try to follow those kind of lines, and as I get more socially involved here I will try and record that in writing. My wife and I are also planning a book for children based on five cats so we're hoping maybe to get that published.

The worst thing about England for me was that I always felt a lack of an authentic relationship with nature in England. Even when you visit the English countryside, I don't have that intimate relationship with the countryside that I have here. For example, I never felt that I could go fishing by myself – I never felt at home in the countryside – you always feel a bit out of place. So I think I see my return here as spiritually uplifting – just for being here for a longer period than before, and doing my favourite activities. It's been a learning experience in all sorts of ways, for example, supervising the building of the house. The alternative of living in England in retirement would not have suited me – this has been a much more dynamic retirement. ■

ALEXANDRA
SORHAINDO

Alexandra Sorhaindo was a teacher before leaving in 1957 to get married in England at the age of 21. She worked and brought up a family there. Returning to Dominica in 1989 she lives in St Aroment.

I had just turned 21 and was a teacher at the Convent High School when early in 1957 I got a letter from my fiancé, who was studying in England, asking me if I would be willing to come up and marry him. We had originally thought that we would wait until he came back home but I guess that loneliness caused him to ask me to come up. It was a surprise for me because although a lot of people were going up to England at that time, it was the farthest thing from my mind.

Life for me was pretty good. I grew up in Roseau although my father was a planter in Castle Bruce and my mother the village postmistress. At that time many more people lived in town – so you could visit each others' homes. There was always something to do. I was a very happy person, and involved in a lot of youth groups, such as the Young Christian Workers and sports. I liked going to dances, fetes, picnics, spending weekends by the river and by the sea – most things that someone growing up in the Caribbean would do. I had enjoyed my teenage life very well. That's why I had no thoughts of leaving.

My fiancé had been away for three years – he was studying optics – and we had corresponded very regularly by mail. He had already written to my father asking for my hand in marriage. And I had said "yes", not knowing what I was letting myself in for. I had heard a lot of England but had no knowledge of what it was going to be like.

We had a teacher at the Convent High – I was educated there and attained my Cambridge advanced level examination – whom we called a walking encyclopaedia. She was a nun from Belgium, but she knew a lot about English history, and was interested in the arts. We read Shakespeare – and the English poets. So I knew about England from that point of view. We grew up with patriotism for England – we celebrated Empire Day and the Queen's birthday. We considered England the mother country...so going to England was like going home to the motherland.

My father gave me his blessing but he and my mother were a bit concerned – I was the first one in the family going to England. I had never travelled away from my parents and I knew no Dominicans in the area where I was going – Bradford, in the north of England, where my fiancé was. I was also apprehensive about my fiancé. Will we have the same love for each other? Will he have changed? He didn't tell me much about his life in England – but he seemed comfortable there and figured I would be as well. I guess I was a bit naïve: I'd just go up to get married and soon I would be back in Dominica. I had no thoughts about how long I would be up there.

At that time, a lot of people were going to England. We used to go down to the Bay Front to see everyone leaving, everyone crying – husbands, wives, boyfriends, parents. It was such a scene when the boat came. Some didn't know what they were going to – some just with one suitcase, and very little cash. There were always lots of tears every time people left.

Two of my friends were going up at the same time, one to go on holiday, one like me to get married. We went on the French boat, the *Colombie*. We shared a cabin and had a very enjoyable experience. I wasn't one to get seasick. It was like a holiday at sea. I didn't think of what I was going to face in England.

The boat docked in Southampton. It was the first of April 1957, and I never lived that down because when I started working all my English friends said, "Oh my goodness, you must have been an April fool to leave all that sun and come to this country." When we stepped out on deck the air was cold, and when we spoke we saw this vapour thing came out from our mouths and that was strange to us; and then we looked up to the sky and what seemed to be the sun was just a little thing in the sky. In fact, one of the guys on the boat shouted "Mon Dieu, their sun's smaller than ours", and we all started to laugh. Our first glimpse of misty, grey, dull, wet, cold England and we thought oh my goodness is that what we have come to.

My fiancé and I had to have a special licence to get married because I hadn't been in the country long enough. So I had to rush up north to Bradford and I must say that when I got off the train and looked out, I saw this...grey...I can't describe the buildings...I thought oh my goodness. And I think I would have stayed on that train and gone right back, but I saw my husband-to-be at the barrier and that changed my mind.

In Bradford, I had my first experience of living in lodgings, in what they called a bed-sitter, sharing the kitchen and bathroom. That was a very, very new and strange concept to me. The landlady and landlord were my first introduction to English people – well we had people from Britain in Dominica, the governor and civil servants and so on, so I knew white people but I didn't really mingle with them, and the nuns in the convent were Belgian. But coming to England where almost every face was white that was different.

When my fiancé, who was fair skinned, first went to look for lodgings he had gone with a friend, who was very very dark. Almost every house they knocked on, when the door opened, they said sorry no vacancies. So he said to him, I think I will try on my own and see what happens. That was the first time that it really hit him that it did matter what colour your skin was because when he went on his own the people were more receptive and he did get accommodation. So that was a bit of a shock.

In Dominica there was a lot of class prejudice but race and colour was not so much that we thought of. But in England, when I went to the employment agency, the young lady who interviewed me said that there were vacancies for office work and did I mind if she told them I was coloured. I didn't think much of that, it didn't matter to me, not realising that it did matter to the people who were going to employ me. But fortunately I got a job in the office in Listers, a large mill in Bradford. I was the only black person working in the office. I enjoyed my job very much – and I was respected for what I did. Again I don't know if it is because I take people as I find them… I didn't have a chip on my shoulder, but I must say they were very, very nice to me. When I was expecting my first baby, I got very sick and we had to move into a new flat, and it was the white girls who cleaned it, scrubbed it and put up my curtains for me because I had no coloured friends or family there.

Well I never felt racism at work – even if they thought it, I never felt it. But I remember once going to a pub with my husband and an English couple and the landlord was not very polite to me – I must have been the darkest in the group. So we just walked out. I never encountered harsh racism though I know it existed. I heard a lot of stories about racism – even that people were told to find another church, and when I heard that I was appalled.

Soon after getting married I was expecting our first child and because of that we were able to get a council flat, which was much

Early life in Bradford in the north of England. Her marriage to Martin Sorhaindo, then a student, was noted in the local newspaper.

Bride from the West Indies in Bradford

TODAY'S bride at St. Patrick's Roman Catholic Church, Bradford, Miss Alexandra Stephenson, came to England recently from Dominica, in the West Indies, for her marriage to a fellow-countryman, Mr. Martin Sorhaindo, who is in his fourth year as a student at the Bradford Institute of Advanced Technology (formerly the Technical College). They are

better, in a very nice area but it was far from the city so I didn't do much socialising at that time. Much of my time was occupied with the family. We always explained to the children about the lovely things about home – the trees and the fruit – so they grew up knowing about Dominica. Mostly we cooked English dishes – you could get some Dominican provisions but they were always more expensive; it was easier to get potatoes and rice. We told them it was our intention to go back.

I kept in contact with my family and friends by letter and although I missed Dominica I was quite happy being with my husband and my children. However, my husband felt he would be better off serving his own people. He had a great love of country and he thought that as soon as possible, when he was financially secure, we would go back home. So in December 1966 – by then we had three children – we sold our house and went home. I was really looking forward to going back – longing to see my mother, father, brothers and sisters. I wanted them to see their grandchildren. I had never visited Dominica in those years – it was expensive and travel was by boat not by plane.

We had a lovely boat trip back, more like a cruise. We went to Lisbon, Madeira, Curaçao and Jamaica and stopped at all those places. There was dancing almost every night, and deck tennis. There were some Dominicans on the boat who had been in England studying, mostly teachers.

When we got to Dominica it was night time and in those days there was no deepwater harbour; you had to jump from the big boat into a little boat and that was quite frightening. But I was so happy when I got on the jetty and saw my brothers and sisters and friends – and one shouted, "Oh Alix hasn't changed at all." That made me feel quite good.

When we first came back I didn't think much about politics, but soon after we got a little disenchanted with the government and the different laws that were being passed. I didn't think my husband was politically minded but I soon saw that he was. He went on to the town council, became deputy mayor of Roseau, and then a new party was formed, the Dominica Freedom Party, and he became its first general secretary. He even went up to represent a constituency during the election of 1975. He always stood for justice and people's wellbeing.

At that time not many were returning home. The only ones were those who had gone specifically to study or train. I didn't feel as if I'd ever left. I fell into the laps of my friends and being a teacher there were lots of pupils and parents. I'd maintained contacts and I think I fitted in well. Nobody saw me as someone who had come back from a strange country; I was just welcomed back with open arms.

The children adjusted well into life in Dominica – the eldest got teased for his English accent when he first went to school so he soon made an effort to get the rankest Dominican accent you could think about. My husband opened a practice in Roseau and I stayed home with the kids for almost a year and then returned to teach at the Convent High school. By that time my husband said he wanted a Dominican-born child – he got twin daughters and was very proud about that.

After some years, my husband more or less decided that we had to go back to England. He didn't discuss it much with me, but he was thinking of his children's further education, and felt that politics was taking up too much of his time and money. So he decided to sell the house and go back to England although he had said that he wasn't going to go back. It was circumstances that forced him to make that decision.

So in 1976, just before independence, he applied to his old firm in Bradford but there were no opportunities for him there. But they had just bought a new practice in Ipswich, in Suffolk, and asked him to go there and manage that practice. So that was it and it was off to England again – this time by plane. I really didn't want to go back – I was happy in Dominica and enjoyed my teaching. I remembered cold Bradford, the snow and more snow. And I had never heard of Ipswich.

Ipswich was a little town, very, very flat – there were no hills, not like Bradford. My first impression was that I didn't really like it but it was a quaint little place. Suffolk people, I got to know afterwards, don't take kindly to strangers, it doesn't matter whether you're black or white. Another thing that struck me was that there were no Dominicans there at all – so we couldn't socialise with Dominicans. Eventually we found one Dominican from the same village as my husband who was married to an English woman. In fact, there were not many black people in Ipswich at that time. Later there was a larger influx.

They weren't employing any more teachers at that time so I applied to join the civil service, and got a job in Ipswich in the tax office as a clerical assistant – again I was the only black person there – where I worked for about 11 years. I missed not being able to teach – I'd never done clerical work before but I got to like my job and the people I worked with were very kind to me, even the bosses. My husband enjoyed meeting people and he had a very good influence on a lot of people too.

The three elder children were able to go to the top grammar school in Ipswich, and the two younger ones went to the junior school, close to where we lived. For our eldest child it was a very, very traumatic experience – he was just ready to go to sixth form, at an age when it is not easy to make new friends. He felt that very much. The two other children were also teenagers; and they experienced a lot of racial tension at school so their school life was not very happy. They didn't talk about it very much so we were not aware of that at the time.

We always taught our children to be proud of the fact that they were black and to remember that if you are the only black person in a crowd of white people you are going to be spotted and to make sure to be on your p's and q's and to do what was right. If someone picked on them for the colour of their skin that's OK but make sure that no one could pick on them for their behaviour – so I always made sure that they maintained the best behaviour possible.

My life was mainly at home with the children although I did get into groups at my church so I met people then. Ipswich suited me fine. It was a quiet place, and I got to like it. There were quaint little villages on the outskirts, and on my day off I used to go on bus trips here and there. I was able to visit Constable country: my teachers had told us so much about the paintings of Constable and to actually see the places – Flatford Mill, Dedham – that was really exciting.

Then, in 1979, there was Hurricane David that hit Dominica very badly, and we did a lot of work collecting contributions to send back. We felt very sad about all of that. In fact someone rang my husband and said that his house was one of only three with its roof on in St Aroment. We felt very sad because we were so far away. We did a lot of work collecting donations.

My parents were still alive so I always had that yearning to go back to Dominica. When I used to go on holidays I would say I'm going home, and my work mates said, "This is your home." But I said, "No, I live here but Dominica is my home." England was the place I lived and to make the best of what I could but to me Dominica was home. I thought maybe I would stay there until I would retire – I had plans for learning to paint and to play the guitar.

Then my husband suffered a back injury and it became very difficult for him, especially with his profession and the cold weather, and he didn't feel he could stay in England. He tried to get early retirement from his company but they wouldn't allow it so he had a very, very rough time. He was determined that if he stayed in England his health would get worse – and he was keen on gardening and fishing, and you couldn't do very much of that in England. I, too, tried to get early retirement but I just had to resign. That was hard.

I couldn't see him spending another winter in England so in 1989 we had to sell up and go. While we were packing to go back to

Dominica – we had already sent most of our things in a container – we heard on the radio that Hurricane Hugo was approaching this tiny island of Dominica which had suffered so badly from Hurricane David. And I thought God! Don't let that happen to us. Our container was on the high seas, we didn't have a house in England, we had bought a house in Dominica and I thought that would be destroyed. But fortunately Dominica didn't get too much of a bashing.

I was really looking forward to going back home…because I felt my husband wanted to go back and I thought it would do him good. The children couldn't come with us – two were married by then and we had grandchildren. That was a hard decision. We came back with a much reduced pension but that was the sacrifice we had to make.

When my husband got off the plane he took off his tie, knelt down and kissed the ground and said never again would he leave Dominica. He was so happy. He set up his practice and although I was asked if I would go back to teach I noticed that the young people weren't the same – they were more influenced by western society and less respectful. So I decided not to go back to teaching but to help in my husband's practice.

To be honest, I feel that the kids never forgave us for going back to England. They really enjoyed being in Dominica. They had got so at home there – able to run about, go to the river, fish, go the sea, climb trees. And the basic education is better in Dominica – the teachers are more strict and children at that time grew up being more respectful so it was very good that they had that time in Dominica. I think because of our social background in Dominica they might have grown up with a greater sense of self worth instead of going to a country where you are regarded as second-class citizens. My children are all proud of being black, one of my daughters does a lot of work with black communities in Ipswich.

❝When we come back home we shouldn't think that we are better than those who are there. We should accept them, love them and live harmoniously with them because we are all Dominicans after all.❞

But I'm happy for them, too, because they have lived in both worlds so they knew what it was to grow up in Dominica and to live in England whereas many children born of West Indian parents don't have that opportunity. So I think our children have a greater sense of pride in being West Indian than the average child of West Indian parents born in Britain. I always said that if I had a lot of money I would give every child born in England of West Indian parents the opportunity to go to the West Indies and see what it is like. Because they grow up in England, and never see the Caribbean, they get a false impression of what it is. And unfortunately a lot of West Indian parents do not teach their children to love their West Indian heritage. I think if those children had a greater sense of who they are and where they came from, they wouldn't get in so much trouble. They should have pride in being West Indian and being black and let no one tell them different.

I know that a lot of returnees to Dominica find it hard when they return. Again, it's a two-way switch – you have to give and take. When you stay in England a long time, there are certain things you get accustomed to and when you get back to Dominica you expect it to be the same but it's not the same so you get frustrated. Things frustrate you like the slowness of people in business – slow to attend to customers and slow to act but you can't have everything. One should come back with an open mind … taking things as you find them. Don't expect people to welcome you with open arms, especially if you've stayed away for many years and not kept in close contact. Then it can't be easy, it's like going back to a foreign country and you get treated like a foreigner.

I enjoy the sunshine most of all – not having to wear so many clothes, and to be among people you know, who love you and accept you. That makes a difference. Leaving my children and grandchildren in England was the hardest. But I make trips to England just to see them, and fortunately we are a very close family and they visit me regularly and that helps a lot. I've been back nearly 20 years – I have no regrets. I was never regarded as a stranger come back – I don't think people see me as a returnee.

I've heard some returnees say that some Dominicans treat them differently – I think a lot of people in Dominica have this false idea that because you live in England you have tons of money. They don't know that when in England you have to work very, very, very hard for every penny. Sometimes I tell Dominicans when relatives send them barrels and I see them abuse the things that are sent to them, I say to them, "Listen you don't know how many jobs that person has to have to send you this barrel. You have to appreciate it and not take it for granted." I think that's one bad thing many Dominicans have – they think that because you come from England you should just hand things over. I wish they would change that concept.

More and more people are returning. It's a good thing because they are contributing to the economy of the country. They are not relying on Dominica because they are getting their pension and contributing. A lot of returning Dominicans have skills that can be put to good use to help Dominica. As my husband said, he could use his skills for his countrymen.

I encourage our people to come back with an open mind, not to come back thinking I've been in England for many years so I'm better than the people who were in Dominica. A lot of the people who we left in Dominica have come up in society much better than some of us living and struggling in England. It's difficult to explain – sometimes moving to England has not made us better; in fact, some of us would have been better off if we had stayed in Dominica. When we come back home we shouldn't think that we are better than those who are there or think that we know more than they do. We should accept them, love them and live harmoniously with them because we are all Dominicans after all. ■

CLAYTON
SHILLINGFORD

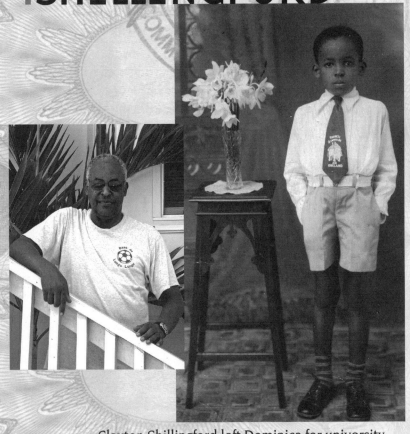

Clayton Shillingford left Dominica for university
in Jamaica in 1957. He spent much of his
working life in the United States as an expert in
tropical agriculture for the multinational
Dupont company. He is president of the
Dominica Academy of Arts and Sciences and
returned to Dominica in 2000.

When I was a boy, all the schools on Empire Day had to go and drill in the Botanic Gardens. And there was this song, Rule Britannia, with the words, "Britons never, never shall be slaves." Even at a young age I thought that there was something not quite right about this. How come they can't be slaves, but they want to have everyone else in slavery. There was a kind of subservience – people had pictures of the then king and queen in their homes – of let's go along with the flow of the colonial system. For example, my mother got me a tie for my first communion (*photograph*, *left*), which said, "There will always be an England."

I didn't like the idea of all that and part of the reason why I was never very deeply religious was because of the way I saw the system operate. For example, in the cathedral, you couldn't go and sit in certain pews because they had little metal things with someone's name, and those names – McIntyre, Bellot, Blanchard, Burton, Nicholls, even Shillingford, my own name – created in me a sense that something wasn't quite right. All those families lived near the cathedral, but my home was in Hillsborough Street and the further you were from the cathedral, the lower the status of the people. It was very, very clear to me what I was challenged with: on one side, my father, Thomas Hesketh Shillingford, who belonged to that sector of society and living up that side, and then my mother, who came from Mahaut, who lived towards the river in Roseau, not the select areas. I'm between the devil and the deep blue sea so to speak.

When my father would come over from Grenada where he was working in the Shillingford lime factory, I couldn't go and see him when I wanted because my paternal grandmother would be at the door saying when I could come and when I couldn't come. There was a lot of racial prejudice about little black boys, that kind of nonsense, and a bias, too, against people who came from the country. Country-bookie … it didn't matter what your colour was, if you didn't come from Roseau, you were not part of that Roseau group.

My mother was very concerned that I should have the best education – so initially I went to a private school. My mother and dad were not married and I am not sure how she got the money although I know she worked at one time at the Paz shop, and sold food items such as black pudding and crab backs, but I also know that my dad gave her money to help support me. At that time, the island provided one scholarship for the Dominica Grammar School based on an exam from all the primary schools and I was fortunate to get the scholarship. At the grammar school – the headmaster was a white man from England – what we read then was too much of an emphasis on English history and traditions and very little about our own Caribbean history. Even when you went into the sciences, the books we read were published in the UK, and they didn't always have relevance to the natural environment here – for example, there was little or no mention of tropical plants in the botany text books.

Outside school, our interest in our gang was in sport. There was cricket and football, table tennis yes, but no lawn tennis – at least not available to us. There were two clubs, the Union Club, and what we called the White People's Club, and these clubs were mostly

Sporting life in Jamaica: in a football team (kneeling, centre)
at the University of the West Indies, 1961

occupied by the colonial authorities and upper-class persons in
Roseau. So we played sport at the old Windsor Park, at the Gardens
or at New Town – and sometimes we even played cricket in the little
passageways between our homes. The other activity that influenced
us was reading comics, and US movies were very very important to us
and we were always anxious to go to the Olympia cinema – it was
where the Roseau market is now – at the weekends.

I was born in Roseau in 1936 so I grew up during the second world
war. We had problems with food supplies, especially imported food.
We had roasted breadfruit for breakfast because there was not
enough flour to make bread. We did though get imported salted pork
in casks in brine. The meat was very pale and Dominicans began to
say that it was *"bonda Gamand"*, the backsides of Germans killed
during the war. We often saw the German U boats on patrol to
prevent supplies going back and forth between UK and the islands.

I first left Dominica by schooner in 1952 with my half-brother Eric to visit our Dad in Grenada. (Eric died in that fatal carnival fire in 1963.) Then, in 1957, I went to Jamaica, to the University of the West Indies (UWI), to study science on what was called the Commonwealth Development scholarship. Very few left for university then. Jamaica was an eye-opener for me, at the time it was more progressive – in agriculture, in education, and there was all this music, drama, art and dance. That was dominant. So you got exposed to all of that.

When I came back in 1962, I was the senior science master at the Dominica Grammar School. I had mixed feelings about coming back – because I was engaged to a Jamaican, and, secondly, many of the students who graduated at high levels as I did were being offered good positions in Jamaica. But I felt an obligation – in those days when you went to study abroad you had a bond and you'd come back and work in the public service. So I felt I had to come back.

I was also enthusiastic because I felt that I could contribute in the science area because that was so poor. I led the effort to set up laboratories in botany, zoology, chemistry and physics at school and began to build a science programme. Other graduates had also come back, most of them UWI graduates, and we had a very solid faculty. We got the Cambridge examination board to alter the syllabus – to put in Caribbean plants, so you didn't have to study wheat, you could study sugar cane, bananas, coconut and so on.

Even back then there were marks against you when you returned from abroad. Firstly, you were different – and you were – and secondly you were educated and had a degree and not many people had degrees. We were called UWI rebels. We had a different approach and we brought in different ideas about national development. Dominicans were very provincial – indeed, we're not always very enthusiastic about outside influence and interference, which is why we have all the drama about the Dominican diaspora today.

The people who were accepted more easily were the doctors and the lawyers, that was the old tradition, but those who had been scientists and engineers and so on had a different outlook and it created a little friction – and politicians making speeches and saying "*gadé yo*" – "they think they're better than you."

Then in 1966 I made a traumatic departure from the island. One morning, the minister of social services, Wills Strathmore Stevens, barged into the grammar school morning assembly without notice and wanted to give the students some kind of lecture on manners and proceeded to say that the reason why the students had no manners was that the masters' manners were questionable. This was consequent to a booing he got from secondary school students the previous evening at the St Gerard's Hall. I walked out of the assembly with some others – all from UWI – and under colonial rules we were charged by the administrator with gross discourtesy to the minister. The whole thing became ridiculous. The magistrate found us guilty and sent his findings to the administrator who didn't know how to handle it, and sent it to England to the colonial secretary Judith Hart in Harold Wilson's Labour government. But the UK didn't want to lose face and said we should be punished and removed from the grammar school. I was sent to the forestry division. They advised the police that the school was out of bounds and we were not to go near it. After that, I felt that I should get out, and I headed off to Jamaica and quite frankly at that time I had no feeling to return.

I stayed in Jamaica, did my masters in botany in 1967 based on a study I had completed on the Dominican rain forest, and then got a scholarship to study plant pathology and agriculture at Imperial College, London. Then I came back to Jamaica and worked with bananas as senior pathologist in the Jamaican Banana Board research department. In 1975 on a study leave and a research assistantship, I went to the University of Illinois where I completed my PhD in plant pathology in less than two years and returned to Jamaica with my family as director of research of the banana board. But by 1979 the banana industry was in some turmoil and Jamaica was getting a little uncomfortable, there was a lot of crime, and I thought I should take my family and come back here.

My main motivation was to get out of the trouble in Jamaica, and some inducement by some people here, people who were now in power and whom I had taught. Perhaps now, I thought, we could do something together to move the country forward. So I came back in 1979 to be managing director of Dominica Banana Growers Association. But I arrived one day after Hurricane David – the entire place was in a shambles. I was here for about a week and a half. And when I looked at things – the situation was not encouraging. Some people said I abandoned ship but I had a family, my daughter was aged seven and my son, 12. I suppose it would have been possible to stay but a lot of politics got into the thing at the time. So I saw my mother and said, "I'm sorry, Ma, I'm going again." Fortunately for me I had a US alien registration card, and the following day I left for the US on a relief cargo plane.

I was offered a visiting professorship at the University of Illinois, and the next year, 1980, I started to work with the Dupont company as product development manager in Delaware, but I was soon relocated to Miami. The Miami office served all of Latin America and the Caribbean. But I had political difficulties too, in the Miami office, because I was immersed with white Cubans and I was the only person in the company office who had a PhD and was qualified in bananas and tropical agriculture. One Cuban salesman couldn't deal with the idea of an individual from a small island who had a PhD and he decided to give me a hard time.

I worked out of the Miami office up to the end of 1992 during which time I was given development responsibility for banana markets worldwide. During this period I made frequent visits to the Windward Islands and Dominica and was able to keep in touch with my family and national developments.

In the US, racism was there, but Dupont as a global company decided to implement a multi-cultural programme – it was compulsory because you had to know how to talk and relate to people of different cultures. I became president of the Black Employees Network so we were able to help other blacks who had employment problems. It was US law – you couldn't discriminate on any basis. People knew their rights. It was an entirely different atmosphere up there.

I have to say I had more respect inside Dupont than I've had in my own country. America is different – they are very much focussed on let's get things done. When you went to a meeting there was no idle talk. You went to provide a solution to the problems. Even today, if there's an internal problem in Dupont in my field of expertise – they phone me. But my own country are not calling me or asking me anything.

I got a lot of training and a lot of rewards for my work; my salary improved immensely. I sent money mostly to my mother. She was in charge of the family. I also gave her a first trip out of the country – and I took her to Boston to see my brother. So I was able to do these things.

I was often in Dominica through that time – I travelled regularly for work to Latin America, to the Windward Islands, to Jamaica and Belize, and I would be in Dominica four or five times a year. That was

> ❝ If Dominicans want
> to come back, they
> should come. We need
> change and that
> won't come about if
> folks keep their
> mouths shut. ❞

more typical of our people who went to North America – there was that distinction in educational level – and those who went to the US more often went to improve their education, while those who went to the UK went to work. So you had a different group of people. The North Americans had more proximity to Dominica and also were more advantaged in terms of financial capacity so they came back more regularly and maintained their connections.

When I was first in Florida, the Caribbean community in Miami was mainly Jamaicans – there were not many Dominicans in the Miami area but that built up after a while until we were able to form the South Florida Association of Dominica. I was president of the group. We brought up WCK for the Miami carnival for the first time in the mid 1980s, and since that time they have gone up every year. We brought up bands for our fund-raising parties, for independence and all that. We did fund raising not just for Dominicans in the area but also for Dominica itself, sending money, books for libraries, scholarships for high school students, supplies and so on.

I always had the sense that the model we had set up in Miami perhaps could be extended to form an international network. So when I retired in 1998, I received a call from Gabriel Christian and Raglan Riviere, co-founders of the Dominica Academy of Arts and Sciences (DAAS). They said let's start a steering group and we're going to put you in as president. The aim of DAAS is to do charitable work on the island. We built a website and a membership and made connection with Dominican organisations overseas. All this was always focussed on things we could do in and for Dominica.

I always had that sense of coming back and, since I had the wherewithal, I could build a house, and travel back and forth as I want to. I first moved back around 2000 when we formed DAAS. My experience here has been a kind of mixed package. This whole diaspora movement came on the scene just at the time we started DAAS. I feel something is happening in the culture and philosophy of our people – many Dominicans have come back home, started businesses and taken positions of leadership. More people should come – get involved. Everyone should be trooping up to Dominica State College, and offering their services as guest lecturers and so on. Those things are positive.

The prime minister Roosevelt Skerrit asked DAAS to prepare a diaspora policy document, and I presented it in November 2005. There was never any acknowledgement, never a review, never let's meet and see what we can do together. And we have a minister of diaspora affairs – I take that to mean that there is an intention to build a partnership with Dominica's overseas resources but we haven't seen any plan or action.

The difficulty is not the unwillingness of the folks in the diaspora, the obstacles are at this end. One of the factors about coming back is that you have been abroad, you've achieved. There is a little bit of envy, not even at a conscious level. The other thing is that we have a status quo society – they like it where it is; change is too risky. So when you come back you have different ideas – they will attack you and say you can't come and tell us what to do, to the extent that if someone from outside says that there are too many potholes, someone is going to put up a defence of potholes. The other complication, even though we are reluctant to accept critical analysis by our own people, is that if someone comes, say from the European Union, and says exactly the same thing it's not so bad.

Folks who went overseas went to improve themselves – you can't hold that against an individual. It's not abandoning Dominica. There has never in my opinion been any abandonment. We even have people going away today – to the islands, to find employment or study – I can't see what's wrong with that. Look at DUKA, the vision of DUKA is not to follow the British line, the vision is to provide some kind of social network for Dominicans resident in UK to bring the culture even to London. This idea of abandonment is a red herring from my point of view.

All those remittances and the "barrel economy" continue to this day – it's a substantial safety net that our government in some way doesn't want to acknowledge. Some people don't like what I say, but when the medical stores burned down a couple of years ago, the then hospital co-ordinator, who is also a member of DAAS, sent out an SOS to say can you help. DAAS was in contact with two organisations in the US, one called Americares Inc and the other was assembling material for the tsunami in south-east Asia, and there was some surplus drugs and medical equipment. In both cases materials were sent to Dominica in 40ft containers. The folks came from Americares wanting to see how the distribution took place, and I asked the relevant minister of health that letters of gratitude and thanks be sent, but they never were. That is why I have my disappointments.

It's a complex business but we have a culture here that doesn't like to show gratitude. If someone borrows money from you in a tight spot, first of all they don't say thank you, but the worst thing you can do is to remind that person ... you're in dead trouble. They don't

Office life in the United States: working for Dupont in 1996.

want to encourage you, they want to bring you down. It is very unfortunate. These are some of the things that interfere with our relationships with our overseas communities.

When I came here to build this house in Checkhall, the drains were not being cleaned, the roads were bad, there were no lights and so on. So I said, let's see if we can form an association for the community. So we formed the Checkhall Valley Homeowners Association and agreed that everyone puts in $20 a month. When everything was in place, the returnees from the UK continued to pay, the locals stopped. They feel we have the services now, and the UK and other returnees have a big fat pension and so you pay. Someone even wants the government to tax the pensions of the returnees. They don't see how hard it was for folks who went overseas. What they see is that you are here now, and you supposedly have a lot of money. The UK folks get the worst time of all; they really give them a rough time – because of the accent and all that. They start with nonsense about "English", all that foolishness. Some of the folks who return from the UK did make some technical errors to call themselves the expatriates. I don't think that's a good idea; we have to integrate – and not put ourselves in a separate category.

I socialise with people in the community here and my family to a certain extent. I have the interaction with returnees, with Dominicans who visit and my Dominican friends who are resident here. I try to help within the DAAS organisation to bring new ideas, to have a presence in society. Some of the local DAAS members don't want to participate; they are terrified with what the reaction may be. But I say we cannot be doing low profile in our own country.

The positive things are that I've had some influence on political and social dialogue both in a personal capacity and as president of DAAS. Now someone is calling me to ask me about this or that – that was not the case before. That would suggest that something has happened in the nature of the dialogue.

I'm on the board of trustees of All Saints University. If I hadn't come back that wouldn't happen. DAAS also has good connections with Ross University, and the Clemson facility at Springfield. I would wish more than anything else to have a more intimate connection with agriculture – but they will not let me in. However, we have a very good relationship with the National Agriculture Youth Association, and we're helping the Waitukubuli Ecological Foundation.

My children and grandchildren have been coming back now that I have a home here – my daughter has been here a number of times. But I think it's unlikely my children will come and live here. But it's possible that some children who were born overseas will have a sufficient sentiment about the country of their parents to come back. There's a responsibility at this end, too, to make it possible for citizenship for that generation to happen.

If Dominicans want to come back, they should come. We need

change and that won't come about if folks keep their mouths shut. DAAS started trying to partner with the government – but that didn't make any progress. So now we're partners with all institutions, public or private sector. For example, we have put up a wind turbine in the north to see if we can generate energy. We don't have to depend on the government to do these things.

It's very important to try and move our relationship between Dominicans here and overseas. It's perhaps the most important partnership that is going to move the country forward. I believe that it's going to be very difficult to depend only on our local resources to get the kind of progress that is necessary – the challenges are tremendous. We're going to have problems with the cost of living, educating our people, providing services in health and education. And even in respect of having a sporting team representing the country and building our international image. The only reason we were able to hold Barbados at bay in the FIFA World Cup matches was because we had all those footballers coming from overseas – you can even use that as an analogy of the partnership between Dominicans and those overseas – it strengthens our capacity.

The issue about returnees needs to be talked about. In the end, what is going to have an impact are the things you do by example. This will change the situation, as we're able to do more and more things, and become visible. Then you're going to convert people. That's why I'm dead against Dominicans who come here and hide in their caboose, and decide not to get involved, not registering to vote and so on. Even when the power goes off, no one calls Domlec and complains, but I do. You have to do something to change the standards. You don't bring about change by silence. ■

HELENA DURAND

Helena Durand was raised in Wesley and left for England in 1959 as a young woman. She planned to be there for five years – but stayed for 37 years, bringing up three children and working as a nurse. She returned in 1996 and lives in Antrizle with her husband.

I left Dominica on the *Colombie* on September 29 1959 (*her passport
stamp, left*) when I was 23. My brother had sent for me. He paid
for my ticket to go. He had gone to England for a far better life and
you go to try to help the others behind. In the end four of us from the
family went. My eldest brother went and then another brother and
the younger one, the one who sent for me. The elder brother died in
England.

We were from Wesley, and there were 12 of us in the family. My
parents were both farmers, they worked very hard. I went to school at
Wesley primary school and then as I got older I went to sit my exam
and went to Wesley High School. My childhood wasn't too bad at all,
I mean you would expect it to be harder than now: we went to the
spring for water, and went to fetch firewood, but we kind of get used
to it; it was kind of fun. And sometimes Sunday after church, the
whole family go for a sea bath. We were well looked after.

I didn't know much about England: we keep hearing things about
England that the streets are paved with gold, and we were taking it
literally. You'd hear these nice stories and think, oh I wish I could go
there. I was at home, I wasn't really working, and if I get to go to
England I'll get a job and do something better for myself. I had to
leave my two children, my mother looked after them. They were OK;

they were well looked after. There were quite a lot of Dominicans on the boat. Some good, some noisy, some littering and making a mess on the boat. The trip was long, I remember being sick as a dog. I think we docked at Southampton because we had to take a train to come up to Paddington where my brother who sent for me met me. I was quite excited. It was a bit cold; summer was just fading away. Sometimes you have nice weather going into October, but I had to wait for about two weeks until I got my winter coat. It wasn't so bad though. I was living in Paddington – when I got there, I stayed with one of my brothers for little while and then got a room in the same building.

But when I got there, I was kind of disappointed…you're going with this big expectation and you think, oh, is that it? It wasn't long before I got a job in a hotel, working in the kitchen doing the vegetables. It was OK for a while, but from the start I think this isn't what I'm going to do for ever. Then I do little jobs in factories, do this, do that, and then I got out and worked as a nursery assistant. I took a NNEB (National Nursing Examination Board) course and got a certificate. And from the nursery I went into auxiliary nursing with St Charles Hospital, Kensington, in the mental health department. That was what I did for 15 years until I retired.

Working was OK, but sometimes you get a little, no, a lot of aggravation at work. People making you feel like you don't belong, talking amongst themselves and not including you and making you feel uncomfortable. Well most of it was the other staff, not the people in charge or anything like that, but you couldn't say anything. Then I went to work at the Cumberland Hotel. I met some Dominicans there, and talk about bad behaviour. Making *mépwi*, slanderous remarks about each other and arguing with each other. Good grief. I learned more patois in the Cumberland Hotel –

sometimes they forget they were in England and they would not speak English. I wasn't strong in the patois and sometimes I would try and memorise it. And I ask my husband, who is from Petite Soufriere, what is so and so, and he would laugh his head off because I don't pronounce it right. I'm telling the truth, I learned more patois in England than in Dominica.

The English were alright but at a certain time, when you go to look for a job, and they advertise for someone, as soon as they see you they tell you the vacancy is full. It happened to my husband, it happened to me. We had a white friend and we said let's test those people. They did not give us the job, but when we sent in our friend they got offered the job. We got a lot of that. Everyone was complaining but what could we do, you have to learn to live with it.

Then once I stood at a bus stop and I was in the front. The bus is coming. When the bus came, everybody went in and this woman is coming and telling me, wait my turn. Nearly everyone else has gone in. What should I wait for? The next thing the bus is going to pull off and leave me there. And that is what she wanted. You just have to not worry with them.

I met my husband when he happened to come and live in the same building where I was. We got married in Harlesden, in north-west London and then we lived in Paddington and then Wembley. I had three children in England with him. I kept contact with my family and friends in Dominica, especially from the early years. I wrote and wrote …I thought that my fingers would stay on paper. I knew I wouldn't be able to keep it up but I tried my best. When I write it was a pile; at Christmas, I'd send a box to one person and asked him to distribute it. I thought that was nice to keep up with my friends.

I knew my parents were working hard and when I had a few pounds I would send it but it wasn't compulsory. They never forced me to send. I would say that I didn't write because I didn't have anything to send and they said you don't have to have something to send to write. My parents were like that.

We had a lot of friends, and used to go to parties – we had a group from Dominica, Grenada, St Kitts. All mixed. Then the church I went to in England it was like I was here….You probably see only half a dozen white heads and all the rest black so when I went to that church I felt at home. I didn't really have any British friends – I worked with them but not to socialise. I was telling my friends when I came back that I'm sorry I stayed in England for 37 years and you know I only have one white friend, she's Irish.

It was a long time before I got to know anything about the Dominica associations in the UK. I was a member of DONA – I thought it was nice to go and talk about Dominica and if something happening you could contribute. They'd give you newsletters and you could keep in touch with what was happening home. Then, after Hurricane David, my husband worked at McVities, the biscuit factory, at that time, and they organised things to send down.

In England what I most missed about Dominica was the weather, and from time to time I'd dream of the things that we couldn't get over there – not like of late because now there are not much things you can't get in England. I'd dream of things that I'd want to eat. It was ages since I hadn't tasted my mother's cooking.

It was always, always, in my mind that I would come back. I thought I'd stay about five years, but I stayed for 37 years. The money wasn't big and you're trying to save it up and in between you think it's taking so long, so then you break it and go for a holiday and then it take you longer. Remember, too, we were raising the children. Well, after I stayed for about 16 years, I thought, oh my God I must go home. I say this is enough, 16 years, I forget about home. When

Helena Durand and her husband, Octarve, on their wedding day, September 1983, in London.

you're in England, you want to come home, and as soon as you reach back in England, you want to come back again. So after that, I could never stop 16 years before I come home again. When I came that first time it was for about six weeks. My parents didn't think that I had changed. I never picked up an English accent. Then the end of the holiday came; I was so sad but I had to go back otherwise I would lose my job. I came back to Dominica quite a few times. We felt it important to come back and see them all.

At first I used to say that I always want to have the fare saved so that if anything happened to my parents I could come back. It so happened that I had just come down to see them, with all the children and when I'd just come back, my mother took ill. Within a few months she died. It worried me so much, I cried and cried and cried. But I couldn't come back because I didn't have the money.

As the children grew up, they were blaming us for not teaching them patois. I'm not strong in patois but their father refused to teach them because he says they don't teach patois in school. When the children were younger we try and let them have Dominican food, we had to break them in slowly, they had to eat Dominican food as well. For instance, we would say to my son, "You want some rice?" He would say, "What colour?" If we say "brown" it is rice and peas and if we say "white", it is barefoot rice. He preferred the rice and peas. Slowly, slowly we came to introduce a slice of dasheen, a slice of tannia and so. Now they cook their West Indian food.

Then my husband made his mind up – it's home he's coming. I used to go by bus to work, and he used to drive. But mister got more fed up than me and he just said he couldn't take the cold any more. But I was the one taking the cold, standing at the bus stop. But he just wanted to come home – nothing would have stopped him. But from the time I left Dominica, it had been my wish to come back too.

While we were still in England, my husband came down, started this house in Antrizle near Atkinson, stayed a few months, then went back. He come down from time to time to seeing how things going – again it was kind of hard for him because he was self-employed in England. Once when he came down, he said he felt like sitting down and crying – it was just like sending the money and throwing it into the sea. I had to talk to him and say don't worry about it, I had to coax him. The builder wasted material: he asked my husband to buy galvanise and when the house was finished he had 46 sheets of galvanise over. That was an experience no one would like to go through.

We decided to put the house in England up for sale in 1996 and the house sold quicker than we thought. So my husband had to come down in November with the container because the house is sold. In January 1997, I came back.

My children were not happy that I was coming back. One of my granddaughters I used to look after her after school and so on, and when I decide I was coming down, she didn't take it well. We were close. When I left, the mother said she had to take her to the doctor – she said she get things in her head. The doctor said it was the stress because I had to leave. I was so sorry. I did all I could, but I have to come home and have to let her go. My children came down here and visit in 2004. At my last count I had 14 grandchildren.

I didn't really know what it was going to be like coming home. When I first came back I was too excited to find any fault. It was so nice to see my friends again. But after a time, if you come home and have no dealings with the authorities you're OK. But if you have to deal with them, that is when you feel it. Nothing goes smoothly here ... Look I have a coconut tree there. Domlec wants the tree down. They came one Sunday, branch it off and left it. Nobody was here and they didn't ask any permission. My husband said if they ever come back, don't let them put their foot on his land. Well they came back and they cut the coconut tree and go. I call the person who is supposed to be in charge. It took me how many calls to get him. And I say, who is going to pay me for the coconut tree? Are you going to get back to me? If they don't pay me my husband will be mad at me. Things like that gets you.

I'm happy to be back, really – it's only when these things crop up it make you fed up. If you never left here you could probably understand that but when you know how things are done, you've seen it can be another way. Once my husband and I were in Roseau and we were in a snack bar, and we're coming down the step and I'm seeing our jeep is moving without a driver. I say, "Durand, look." A

❝ I don't regret I went to England. That's for sure, and I don't want to say I regret I come home. I just take it as it comes. But things could be better. ❞

woman hit a car and did not stop and kept going and went straight into my husband vehicle. My husband took a lawyer...it go one year, two years, three years, four years. They said the policeman never made a proper report. He never even mention my husband car. It never came to court. In the end, my husband tell the man forget it – he threw in the towel. Those things get you frustrated.

And we go to town and you know how they would call my husband "English". I say have you ever seen a black Englishman? English? They carry on like that all the time. If you see you have an issue, even though you are making sense, don't try to tell them, don't try, just leave them. They'll say, "It's because all you come from England, why all you don't go back?" We born here you know, we come here, why don't we go back where? If you don't want us here where we were born, it's those over there that will want us? They run us from over there, you black this and that, we come home and you tell us to go back. These people are stupid. This you can avoid. Just keep quiet, leave them alone. I should think there is something the government can do to make these people wise up, hold meetings and talk to them, enlighten them.

They handle things much easier in England, with less effort. You can always get someone to sit and talk to if you have an issue. But here you can't tell them anything because you come from abroad. It feels as if you don't belong anywhere. Sometimes they say that we go away, we spend half of our life away and then we come back and build our big houses, fence them up and we stay inside alone. But that's not how we want to live, but that's how they're forcing us to live.

I don't regret I went to England. That's for sure, and I don't want to say I regret I come home. I just take it as it comes. But things could be better. I stayed away 37 years and come back, and there's not much improvement. It would be nice if there was somewhere I could go for a little drink, and meet with other people, have a laugh. I socialise sometimes with other returnees from Wesley. Sometimes we say, let's cook our food at home, go by the beach and bathe. That's nice. But when my husband isn't here, I'm stuck here sometimes. I never learned to drive – I regret it so much. I have to go on the road, and flag down the bus … but I hate that when they pass by straight. I don't know what is taxi, what is what. In Roseau they have dial-a-ride, that's sweet but there's nothing here. Perhaps I'm getting punishment for staying in England so long.

My kids like Dominica, but not to stay, and I cannot blame them. Those kinds of frustrations, I couldn't see them dealing with that. What are they coming here for? Perhaps if there was something for them to do, if they could see an opening, you could encourage them to come: I tell my son, you could try plumbing, electrician, repairing fridges, something like that. But to be honest, I wouldn't encourage the young to come at the moment.

But my wish from the time I left here to go to England, I wanted to come back. Dominica is my home. I cannot say England is my home. I always left with the intention of coming back, and I was very, very happy that God showed me the way to come back.

JANET HEATH

Janet Heath went to England in 1959 when she was six. She worked as a secretary and as a case worker in racial equality. She returned to Dominica with her husband in 2003 and now runs the Titiwi Inn in Citronier.

As a teenager in London, Dominica was in my mind but it was only when I started working and I could save up for my own fare that we were able to return for a holiday. Me, my mum, my sister and brother came back when I was 18 (*photograph, left*). What a culture shock – oh my goodness. You get used to luxury very quickly. First thing was the ravine at Tete Morne, where I had lived with my aunts until I was six. I had forgotten about the ravine – it was like climbing down a precipice and I remember everyone having a good laugh, with me in up-to-the-minute fashion: I arrived in platform shoes in African colours and a mini dress. I refused point blank to go down, and my aunts had to come hop, skip and jump and hold my hand to help me.

And then I remember the house – it was the same house that my parents had left, and my aunts were living in it – it was minute compared to what I remembered. It was like one room, the size of our kitchen in the UK. I remember saying "Where are we sleeping?" My mum told me to shut up because she didn't want me to embarrass my aunts because they were so welcoming and overjoyed to see us. They gave up their room for us to sleep. I remember seeing huge cockroaches – I was so shocked. I just wanted to die, and to get on the first plane home. My uncle lived in Grand Bay off Lallay – he was high up in education and had a huge brick house and I remember demanding that my mother take me there to sleep but she took no notice of me. Then it was so dark at night and my aunts telling stories about *soucouyans* and frightening the daylight out of us.

We were there for six weeks and come the second week it was like I never left. I was running up and down that ravine like everybody. But what I did do was to go to town and bought that Baygon to give to my aunt. My fancy clothes and shoes I couldn't wear again, it wasn't the right place. When we left we were crying, and that visit strengthened my connections with Dominica. I thought then that one day I would return, that I wouldn't die in the UK.

I was born in 1953 and about three when my father went to the UK. My mother went two years later and I went up about a year after that in 1959. I can't remember much about my early life in Tete Morne, but what I do remember are certain smells, and certain plants like *zicack*, the fruit with a hard stone, and the moment I tasted it again I remembered it.

When my father went up to England there were calls for nurses and for people to work in transport – so my father decided that he wanted to see what it was like. His dream was always to come back. He was up there for two years and because he was taking so long to achieve what he wanted to achieve he sent for my mum. It was a time when it was very hard for black people in the UK. For a lot of black people it wasn't the land of milk and honey that they were sold. My aunt, for example, had a brain like a calculator but when she went up she ended up working in a factory.

I have to tell you if my father was born in a different time and with a different skin colour he would have been a Bill Gates, a real entrepreneur. He was one of those people always ahead of his time – although he couldn't really read or write that never kept him back.

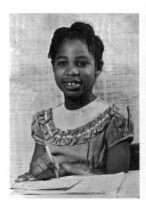

Childhood in London, aged
eight (above), and aged
three, in Dominica before
her mother left for England.

He had a 100% belief in his abilities. When he was in the UK, he did
lots of odd jobs – he was a boilerman, he stoked furnaces and
cleared debris off the trains. He never called anyone to the house: he
was a painter, he did carpentry, the plumbing.

My father bought two houses in London almost straight away –
he paid £400 for them. Lots of family and everyone who came from
our area of Dominica slept in that house – my father would rent the
rooms and once they found their feet then the people would go on
their way. My father was famous for doing that...He was a real
people's person. The people in the house were mainly Dominicans
but not all. I remember a mixed race couple: he was a black guy and
his wife was white, and they had two daughters and he was a
saxophone player. In them days, mixed couples were so rare. My

father loved everybody. He used to go out and bring people back and my mum said, "Where the hell do you get these people from?"

The only thing I can remember about that boat journey to England – I went with my older brother, my younger sister and one of my aunts – everyone was throwing up except me. But I can't remember getting off the boat or where we docked. I never had that conversation with my parents and now I'll never know.

When we first arrived, we rented somewhere in east London – it was one of those huge Victorian houses and we went into some rooms, just round the corner from Roman Road market. Then, shortly after we arrived, we moved to the house my father had bought in Hackney, and I went to the local primary school. When you go to the UK, that's when your friends become international – I knew children from all over the Caribbean and from India. I had a Jewish friend at the bottom of the road; there were Greek children in the street. We all got on – summer times would be a riot. It was a fantastic childhood. I've always been in an environment with different cultures and people. I've never lived somewhere where it's only Dominicans, or only black people.

My school was multi-cultural and I wasn't aware of racism until much later. But I do remember once standing in a grocer's queue with my mother, and there were two little white girls in front of me, and every time I moved closer to them, they moved. I told my mum who said, "Don't take any notice of them, they're just being stupid." But I knew it was because of my colour. I was really upset at the time. My parents just took all that on board – they felt like they were guests in someone else's country. It would be different now.

I don't remember thinking about Dominica until I was in my teens, but I must have missed it because I was close to my aunts, who grew me up and I used to write them and send them pictures of my holy

Marriage, aged 19,
to Keith, in London.

communion. My mum sent them money because they had looked
after us, and also the children of all of my mum's sisters. They really
loved us. They always lived on their own land; they weren't rich but
they were always able to sustain themselves. And the money was the
icing on the cake. Then when I grew up and started working I used to
put a £5 note in a letter. We never lost contact.

In London, we had family coming constantly. My parents were
always Dominicans and talked patois to themselves – although they
didn't believe in talking to us in patois because they thought it'd
hold us back. But we always had that link. There was no question of
not coming down.

I got married to Keith, who is Jamaican, when I was 19. We didn't
come down again until my eldest child was 12. My parents had
already retired and moved back by then – to Grand Bay. My father
built a house there but my mother couldn't settle – she found it too

slow so he bought some land and built this house at Citronier – and my mum was much happier here although she didn't really want to leave the UK. I understand that: she missed her children and grandchildren.

We used to come as often as we could – every couple of years – with the kids and then on our own. I tried to tell my children about Dominica but probably not enough and I was always happy I took them down here even though it was very expensive. But we also had to visit to Jamaica and keep a connection with Keith's side of the family. My kids know they are Dominican: that said, they love coming to Dominica but at the moment they don't say they want to come here to live. Whereas by their age I knew I wanted to come, but for them the ties are not so strong.

From the time we got married, we'd always been planning to come back down when we were 46. I had trained as a secretary – I wanted to be a journalist but in those days it was unheard of, so I went to secretarial college. Later, I did a human resources degree and then in my last three years in London I worked for Enfield Racial Equality Council as an administrator/caseworker. I really enjoyed it and left that job to return to Dominica. You hear stories about people coming back when they are old and dying so we wanted to come back to enjoy ourselves. We also wanted to know more about the Caribbean because we had left when we were so young.

So coming up to 50 we started to buy stuff. We stored and bought, stored and bought maybe for a couple of years. You must have a plan and a back-up. We sorted out the finances and then we had to decide for tax purposes whether it was going to be a clean break; but my children and my whole life was in the UK so, psychologically, I couldn't do that so we decided to have a foot in each camp and to travel between the two.

My children had been hearing about this for so many years but it was a bit of a shock when it came to it. By that time I had my first granddaughter, and if the ball wasn't already in motion, I don't know what would have happened. I find it hard when I visit them and it's even harder when I come back. For the first year, I cried the whole time, I was very depressed. I think I went back about four times that year and then it got less and less. I don't regret the decision but all the things that are happening to my grandchildren, that's really hard – you can't get over that. Telephone calls and emails help but they're nothing like the real thing. But everything else has worked out really well.

My father built this house thinking that we would all come down here and live – so that all his children could come here. I said to him that wouldn't happen but I fully understand that now: I have these rooms here and they all have my children's names on them.

When I came back in 2003 neither of my parents were here – they were back in the UK. My father had been diagnosed with cancer and they couldn't do anything for him here. Before my dad died, he signed over the properties to me and to manage the tenants and stuff. He was really happy that I was going to go back and fix up the house, and it wasn't going to go to rack and ruin. My father would have been mortified if we'd sold it – he really loved owning property and land.

I didn't have any plans past coming here and reacquainting myself with Dominica, although having said that I also wanted to travel the world – and funnily enough to see more of the UK. In 46 years of living there, I had hardly seen any parts of the UK – I'd been to Scotland and Wales and so on for business but not for holiday. And when that sun's shining and England is on form it's a beautiful place. We also thought we'd continue to rent downstairs – but when we

> ❛I think the English
> returnees sometimes
> have a hard time
> because of the English
> thing. They almost see
> us as people who have
> sold out – we've lived in
> the slave masters' home.❜

came, it was in such a terrible state so we took the decision to close downstairs and when we got the money to fix it up, still with the view of renting it.

But having been working in the UK, I'd worked since I was 16 through all my three children – we'd always worked and paid our dues – it's really hard to sit down and do nothing. We found that very difficult. Then round about that time the prime minister was giving a speech about how there weren't enough serviceable rooms in Dominica and how tourists came and there was nowhere to put them, so we thought we have all these rooms and that's how Titiwi Inn started in 2006. After we heard the speech, we said we'd give it a go.

When I moved back I didn't know anybody, I didn't have any friends here. Apart from my cousins, everyone moved away and they wouldn't have remembered me anyway. It's important to be aware of that – that people you left behind may also have left, or died. But what I have found difficult is meeting people my own age or a little bit younger who I can relate to. Social wise I wish it were a lot better – that I knew more people like me, perhaps that's me not making more of an effort to go and find them. But apart from family I can't say that I socialise with many Dominicans. I would like to. I was doing French cookery classes – that was great, a group of five

Dominicans, but then the classes ended. I'm also a member of the Dominica Marine Association – and I've met more new people there. Joining clubs, seeing the country and going out is a way of meeting new people.

I do find it hard to relate to some Dominicans though: we think differently about certain things. Sometimes I hear an English accent and I feel like I'm at home ... and then I get a little confused because I don't know which is home. But then I love the freedom of being here. I can do what I want when I want. It's lovely living here, I don't have any complaints, but I just wish politically that Dominica would develop a bit more, especially for the business we're in. It's very slow. I'm just six rooms but when I open my Domlec bill I can't believe it. I'm paying more for electricity here than in the UK. It's a nightmare. Like everywhere, the cost of living is increasing.

I have a good rapport with my neighbours – the people that you see every day, but sometimes when you go to official places, like the docks, I do have a problem with them. For a start everything is bedecked in multi-coloured tape. And then I used to get into such arguments because they have this attitude towards you because you're from England and have an English accent – it gets their backs up. At first it used to make me angry but now I know how to deal with it. Sometimes you hear Dominicans here talking about English people like they're from Mars. When they realise you're one, they will say the equivalent of an English person saying, "I don't mean you, you're different." I have had that happen to me a few times. I've had people talk patois in front of me thinking I don't understand it, but I do and they get shocked when they realise that I do.

A few things that people say lets you know that they have a real prejudice towards English people in general, but not so much towards American. You can be a Dominican American and you can say what you want and they don't care, but coming out of an English person, that's when they have a problem with it. I think the English returnees sometimes have a hard time because of that English thing. They almost see us as people who have sold out – we've lived in the slave masters' home. And I think that's one of the reasons they don't have problems with US returnees. The thing is the ones from England are more likely to return or visit for weeks on end whereas the ones from America rarely come back. Yet every Dominican must have someone who lives in the UK.

I cannot see myself living in the UK now – when it's in your face you get so used to it, but when I go back now it's not the place that I knew. It's just full of foreigners, although I'm sorry to say that because I was one. When I grew up and they used to say "Too many foreigners", all the black people that were in the UK then, they all worked, they all had a job. There's not many black people that I knew of that were on benefits. And there is a lot of tension, you can feel it when you go up there and it's so expensive there as well. I definitely would not want to be there full time. But I couldn't stay here all the time – I need the two. And my advice for anyone is not to break all ties with the UK, or wherever, until you are absolutely sure this works for you. But Keith is very, very happy here. He goes to the UK but if it were not for the children he would never go. Dominica's a man's country, I think, not in the sense of work because the women are in good positions here and so on, but the men tend to socialise with themselves: if you go somewhere you just see a whole heap of men on their own, don't think twice of bringing their women.

I think more people should be encouraged to return. We need more able bodies, entrepreneurs, people with vision and experience who can work and pay taxes. I don't think the government does enough to encourage that. The government's approach to returnees is that we've all got deep pockets; we've all got money, we're all living the life of Riley. It can look as if the government is only interested in our money rather than our skills. We're viewed as English people who have money. I think they would get more people to think about coming if they said to them your country needs you for this, you've got skills for that and seeing us as Dominicans who can contribute rather than viewing us as the English with the money tree. If they were to say Dominica is a really beautiful place, a beautiful place to bring up your children, and if you have a business overseas think about replicating it here, but no, it's all about the money. When you come down here there's no avenue where you can have a voice without them thinking that we're thinking that we're better than them – we're not better but we have different experiences.

I think Dominica is perfect for anyone who is resourceful. You have to have plans A to Z and you might have to use all of them. I would say, don't get rid of the hopes and aspirations you have, but have them on hold because when you come here you have to tweak them to fit in. Sometimes the differences here can be very demoralising, it feels you're the one whose doing all the holding back to make things work, otherwise you'd be angry all the time. The basic courtesies you don't get here. If someone tells you that they're coming, nine times out of ten they don't come. And they don't say sorry. You just have to accept that.

But that said, I've never found any real problems here. It's been a good move for us. I've always felt myself Dominican, and sometimes when people ask, because of my accent, "Are you a Dominican?" I do feel it's a bit insulting. If I find someone knocking the UK here then I stick up for it. The UK gave me a good life. But underlying all that I've always been a Dominican. ■

FRANKLYN GEORGES

Franklyn Georges left Dominica in 1960 for
England. He became a trades unionist, was the
first African-Caribbean to be elected a councillor
for the London borough of Walthamstow and
served for some years as its mayor (above left). He
returned in 2008 and lives in Salisbury.

As a young man in Dominica, life was – for me – easy. The culture was nice. We had *koudmen* – you want to build a house; you gather your timber, you call the people and the house was built in three weeks. It was a safe life, and whether you were rich or poor you were never a nobody – my parents taught me to respect people, whoever they were. It was that type of society. It was a wonderful.

Of course, the people in the banks were white people, the head of the police, the governor – they were all white. It had an impact, but because I grew up in a middle-class society, it didn't worry me. I felt nobody could stop me from doing anything. It did have an impact on many people – but strangely because I never had to search for work in Dominica it didn't have an impact. But when I reached to England, and looked back, I saw the impact. I don't believe in the word class – that's one word I don't like in Dominica, and racism – that's a word I don't like in England. Those two words have provoked me all my life.

I was born in Guadeloupe in 1937 where my father was working as an agriculturalist. They brought me back to Dominica at the age of about five. Both my parents came from La Plaine but I came back to Roseau. In those days they had no roads in Dominica. Strange but I lived until a big man in Roseau, went to England, came back and never been to La Plaine. I was brought up in St Joseph and in the

Layou Valley heights. My father had two smallholdings one at Gould and the other at Crown, and he was also a supervisor at the Hillsborough tobacco estate.

I went to primary school in Roseau for a short time and then to St Jo primary school, but I left Dominica again to go to Trinidad, to the Caribbean Training College. I went there to study, hoping one day to be a Seventh Adventist preacher but it didn't happen: if I had been a preacher I might have been one of those who said, "Do what I say, not what I do." I stayed in Trinidad until I was 18 or 19, then returned to Dominica and worked at the Bulletin newspaper as an apprentice. I learned the trade as a printer – I did paper cutting, machines, worked on the stone, I did everything. The money wasn't bad in those days – I got about £5 a week.

But we were middle class. Life wasn't too bad – we had people working for us, we had a property in town. I didn't go to England because I had to go, but every day my friends were leaving. Dominica could have been pushing a lot of people, but with me it was that my friends were going. You see there was no work; they were going for a better chance. But with me, I was getting lonely.

I woke up one day, and said to my Dad – we were very close – that I wanted £75 to go to England. He went to the bank and gave it to me. Some people had to save for years for their ticket for the boat. That was 1960. I went to get a passport – at where Fort Young Hotel is now – then I went to Whitchurch and I bought my ticket and was on my way. I had a friend in England, and I told him I was coming.

The boat, the SS *Venezuela*, was nice: it took 21 days. We had an adventure – it was like cruising. We made new friends. There were other Dominicans on the boat – we were all migrating to the UK but we didn't know to exactly where. There was good feeling of hope. We went to Martinique, Trinidad, and Venezuela and then spent a long time at sea. The boat went to Barcelona, and then to Italy. Then we took a train, a ferry across to Dover, then straight to Victoria station.

People thought England was paved with gold – we thought we'd go for five years, make our kill and come back home. It was mostly economic – people were very proud, they wanted to do something with their life. People in England were saying come. There was work at that time – buses, hospitals, schools.

Before I went to the UK, I would say that I knew more about the UK than the ordinary working-class person in England. For example, I was taught the geography of England and some of the people when I asked about a place, they wouldn't know. I learned more about England than people who went to school there.

It was December when we reached England. My very good friend, Amos Giraudel, was there waiting for me – he had a coat for me. I just had one suitcase. I stayed in the East End, very close to Cable Street, in Aldgate East. It was rented accommodation – an ordinary little terraced, three-bedroom house.

It was then that I got the first shock of reality. When we went upstairs, I asked him, "Where are we staying? In the other room?" And he said, "No, this is the room." I was living in a room with three other people. I never had that in my life. Our cooker was on the landing, our toilet was outside. There was no central heating, no double glazing. The streets were very gloomy. There were chimneys all over the place; in those days, too, they had fog.

To me I went back in time – my standard of life went back, not just in accommodation but with everything. That was a kickback. If I had the money I would have jumped on the next boat home. That wasn't the England that I was looking for. I cried – I wanted to go back home. I was very lonely – no mum, no dad.

I had not been nervous at all travelling, but I got nervous when I got to my friend's home. My friends were working so I got up alone. They said if you go out make sure you have a key. For the first two days I was in. Then I went to the labour exchange. I asked about being a printer – they said it was a closed shop so I couldn't get into that at all. I said I would take what was going. I got a job as a labourer in a factory in Commercial Street. I stayed there for about five to six years. It was quite good, and they had a cricket field, and a good cricket team. A director came up to me and said, "Do you play cricket?" and I said, "Yes I do." He said, "Come and play with us on Sunday." I got some whites and went and played, and did quite well. The boss liked me, and it gave me opportunities to get to know the bosses, to mix.

But I had an experience there that I will always remember. One day they sent me to clean up a floor – three white guys and myself – and we all swept the floor and came to the middle. When we got to the middle, the three of them disappeared. I said to myself, I'm not picking that up – in those days you leave one job and get another job, but I'm not walking away either. So I divide the rubbish in four, cleared mine, and went down to the foreman, Eddie, an Italian, and said, "Eddie, it's up to you, you can sack me, do what you want, but you sent four of us to clean that floor, and when we got to the middle, the white guys leave me to pick it all up. I pick up mine." And he looked at me, he was quite surprised for a black guy to say that. And he went and got the other three and said, "You all come pick up the rest." They didn't like that at all. They got angry but I stood my ground. And a week or two after, Eddie came and said, "I'm looking for a charge hand." And he made me a charge hand. That was my first experience of racist problems in England.

After that, I went and got a job as a storekeeper. Then I went to work in a little chemical factory in Stratford; I did that for a short while but didn't enjoy it. Then friends said, "Come and work in a gas works. That money's good." But when I passed the yard – I saw two elderly white gentlemen, and they were coughing. I said, "What's that?" They said, "It's bronchitis." I said to myself I don't think I can do this. From there, I did work as a machinist, and after that at Ford's, Dagenham, for two years on the assembly line. I enjoyed it.

Outside work, I had a very good life. I had friends; the money was good. But my life start changing when I left – it was the 1970s – and went to work on the buses, and became a bus conductor at Barking garage in east London. That was the first place I got involved with a trade union, the Transport and General Workers Union. We had some sort of an action there once which the black guys weren't pleased about. I told some of the boys, this is rubbish, we can't stand for that, we're going to have to represent ourselves. So we had a decision that day – we wanted something and went to the shop steward, a white guy, but he wouldn't do it so we had a meeting, and the boys said, "Frankie, do you want to represent us?" We had to take unofficial action, both black and white, and that Saturday, not one bus left the garage. And from that day, the shop steward was second fiddle. But the manager and I start not seeing eye to eye. He didn't want me there at all.

I next went to work in the Post Office, and stayed there for about three years; then I became itchy, and wanted to have a trade. So I applied to the General Electric Company who used to install telephone equipment. I went there as a labourer and got the opportunity to train. I enjoyed it. I was doing something useful. Once, they sent me to Somerset to install some equipment, and when I got to Taunton, the installer made a few phone calls to find me some digs. But when I reached the first one, they said the place has just gone. I went to the second one, it was gone, too. I didn't go to the third one. I went back to the office and said, "Excuse me, I came here to work, not to muck about. You either get me somewhere to sleep or I'm going back to London. I am not putting up with it." So he asked an Irish lady if she had a place, and put me there.

Back in London, in Walthamstow, I went on a training course in maintenance engineering. That's where my whole life changed. I got a job as a semi-skilled, and later, a skilled fitter at Moorfields Eye Hospital. The union there was the National Union of Public Employees (NUPE) – they had lot of staff, domestics, nurses – most of them black. The branch secretary was a white chap and, to me, he never defended these people aggressively enough. So after a time, I joined NUPE, became a shop steward, then the chairman of the branch at Moorfields, and then I started representing nearly everyone. When the next election came up, the branch secretary knew that he would be knocked out so he stood aside. And I became NUPE branch secretary of three hospitals.

The avenue of trade unionism was open for me. I went on and became the national committee member, for London. This was the 1980s, when Margaret Thatcher was prime minister, and it was a difficult time for the workers. By then, probably 95% of my time was spent on union work – I was at meetings left, right and centre. I became a NUPE health committee member. I worked hard, and I said let me become a fulltime officer. But when I applied, I found racism again. I didn't get through, and I couldn't see why. Other people who hadn't worked as I did became a fulltime officer. So I went to the hospital manager and I said, "I cannot work for an organisation which I believe is racist. I applied for a job with the union, and didn't get it because of the colour of my skin." He said, "Don't leave, stay and work with us." But I decided not to, and went to Haringey council as its industrial relations officer.

At that time, NUPE had one black officer – my mentor, Bernie Grant, later a Labour MP. I said to myself, if you are there, I will be there. We formed the black trade union solidarity movement in the early 1980s, so that if one member was having trouble in one place we would move in and fight. I put a resolution in conference that we should have a race equality officer and we did get that. We did some very good work together, but I left the union because I thought there was racism within it. The people I was doing it for didn't want me – I couldn't work like that.

While I was still with NUPE, one officer suggested I become a local councillor. So I joined the Labour party, and went up to be a councillor in Waltham Forest – they selected me, but gave me a seat in a very strong Liberal party ward. When I reached there, I looked at the selection panel and said, "If you choose me, I will not accept. I belong to Leytonstone, and they sent me to Leyton. Leytonstone is a safe Labour seat. If they want a black man on the council, they should select me for Leytonstone."

When I went back to my ward, I told them that if you want me, you'd better get me a safe ward. One of the three white people who had been selected said, "I'll stand down, and let Frank be selected here." I was selected for Leytonstone and became the first African Caribbean to be elected in the borough of Waltham Forest. That was in 1986, and from that year, Waltham Forest was a changed borough. I forced them to set up a race relations committee – and I became chair of it. I enjoyed working there. I made changes. It was a borough with a lot of black people, but it had no black people in the establishment. When I was first elected, I was going to the members' room and an officer of the council, said, "Excuse me, can I help you? This is the councillors' room." I looked at him and said, "I am Councillor Georges." They'd never had a black councillor before.

With his wife, Veronica. "I felt comfortable in the UK but I knew it wasn't home."

I was on the personnel committee – I became the chair – because I saw there were black manual staff but no black people upstairs or in power. I pushed issues and said I needed black officers. The officers used to do all the short-listing for the interview panels – they would put a stallion up with donkeys. I said I refused to sit on any panel unless I can be on the short-listing panel myself so we could do our own short-listing. Because of that change, the head of housing was a black guy, so was the director of leisure and deputy head of finance. It was an important achievement.

At the end of the first term, the mayor said would I like to be his deputy. I said sure. But because I was deputy I couldn't do much work in my own ward, and I wasn't selected back. But I kicked hell again and they gave me a safe ward. I won, and said I'm going to be mayor – so I became mayor for 1990-91. It was good to put myself up. I was a role model – I did it for the children. I went to all the schools; I started black history month in the borough; we had the Afro-Caribbean carnival. I enjoyed myself.

But then we start fighting again – because the things I wanted to do they didn't want to do. The last year I was mayor, in 1993, I resigned from the Labour party. They saw me as a radical. I said I'm not belonging to you no more, I'm going independent. I wanted to have a Caribbean centre – I got it in the end but I drove through hell to get it. I wanted different things – I said I cannot stay with you hypocrites, and resigned. That was very bad for them because they had a majority of one. Me. I fought them to the bitter end.

I was the first African-Caribbean councillor in the borough, the first African-Caribbean chair of a council committee, the first African-Caribbean deputy mayor and the first African-Caribbean mayor. And one of my achievements was to achieve a "charter mark" that they give to organisations for excellence in public customer service. My committee was safety and public protection – I was chair of that. It gave me great pleasure to receive the award from Prime Minister John Major. It was the first "charter mark" Waltham Forest ever received, and it was my committee that got it.

I left politics then, but I helped the community doing voluntary work for a long time – and I did a lot of work for the Dominica UK Association and the Dominica Overseas Nationals Association, but I had had no connection with Dominica for 30 years although I had always missed it. I think the word is not exactly shame, but I felt I didn't do nothing to come back home – I came from a professional family: my grandfather was the first inspector of schools, my aunt was a teacher, my uncle, Telford Georges, a lawyer, my father, an agriculturalist. For a time I felt I couldn't go back. But I had made my own way – and achieved my own way of life in the university of the world. I did my own thing...but I always wanted to come home.

When I met my present wife, who is from Antigua, she said, "Have you been home at all? Have you had communication with your family?" I said no. She got my sister's address in the United States and then I started writing to her, and then got in touch with my dad. My dad was so happy and I started writing to him and talking to him.

My first trip home was in 1990 – I took a party of kids back home to Antigua and Dominica. I was mayor of Waltham Forest at the time, and we had red carpet treatment in both Antigua and Dominica. That's how Dominica and Antigua got twinned with Waltham Forest. Those two weeks created a feeling to come home. My wife made it a duty that we came every two years and I re-established myself. If someone stays away for many years, it's the worst thing they can do because you become a stranger. I say thank God to my wife, because otherwise I would never have come back home.

My heart, my body, my soul from 1990 was always in Dominica – my mind had no control over it…It was just home and nothing could be better. But I say now, never let your heart take over your mind. You must know what you're coming to. Don't fool yourself.

I lived in England for 40 years, and got used to a particular standard of life. I was blessed that I lived in a very nice area, Waltham Forest. I had a beautiful home, garden, everything. You don't want to show off when you come back, but my dream was to take that same home back here. When you come home, they tell you that you will be able to bring your things down duty free, but it's not like that. I did not realise the expenses we would have.

The other thing I don't like is that when I come back home I'm called an Englishman. I lived all my life in the cold; I've been called a black bastard, a nigger, all kinds of things. Then when I come back home I'm called an Englishman – in my own country. I won't answer them. Excuse me, that I will not accept. I blame plenty of Dominican

> ❝ If it's the last thing I do it is to form an organisation so that returnees have a voice with government so that we can dialogue and tell them what we're missing, what we want... We're saying that we have built this country just as the people who stayed have built the country. ❞

politicians for not educating the local people enough – they have put a division between us and them.

There's also envy. Local people think we just come here and ask for things that we shouldn't have. The politicians never let them know what we, as returnees, have given this country. Each and every one of us who come back here brings a minimum of about EC$50,000 a year in pensions. And when we were in England, we were a social security for this country – we looked after our family, we sent children to school, we build homes for our parents. In DUKA and DONA, we worked hard and sent money down.

Then, when we come back here, the majority of us invest some EC$400-500,000 in building our home; not just that, but it's foreign exchange we've brought in without Dominica raising a finger for it. Local people are not told that – and there is resentment.

When we come back too many of us suffer in isolation. The sad part is that some people go back to England – they can't stand it. That's tragic. They feel unwanted. And if they feel unwanted, their children will feel unwanted. So if we go back and tell the truth to our children, in about 15 years when we pass away, all that our kids will do is to sell the damn property and bring the money back up to England. The connections will be broken.

You used to be able to get a passport down the generations, but the government changed that. My son has got his Dominican passport, but my grandchild cannot get it. So my grandchild will say, "What the hell am I going down there for?" Already, the young generation are not coming here – they are going to Africa or Europe. Africa is giving them opportunities. They say, "Come home." My son has taken this step – he has gone to Ghana, not to Dominica.

I should be able to say to people in England, yes, come back home, but I am not going to say that, I'm going to say, think about it, make sure before you do, not because I suffered but because it's important to know what will happen. For example, your first port of call is the port. When I went there, they wanted to charge me €C$50,000 for my car, more than its value. I also felt very much a foreigner in my own country because the officer asked me for my passport and it says place of birth Guadeloupe, and then I had to show him my father's birth certificate, which says place of birth La Plaine. It seemed he deliberately queried my identity.

If you go to America and come back you're still a Dominican, but we who go to England aren't. If you drive round the island, where you see wealth they are the returnees from England – but local people don't see the work, the tribulations, the racism we experienced. And I am angry about that. Why should I go to England, live 46 years there, achieve a certain life and come back to Dominica and live in a shack, and lower my standard of living in order to be identified as a Dominican, and to be accepted? I totally disagree with that.

If it's the last thing I do it is to form an organisation – non-political and non-religious – in Dominica so that returnees have a voice with government so that we can dialogue, and tell them what we're missing, what we want. We need an association where government can meet with us and discuss our needs – at the moment they meet with themselves and tell us what we are allowed. I believe the time has come that we should dialogue with them, tell them what our gains are over there, and what are losses and gains are here. We're saying that we have built this country just as the people who stayed have built the country.

The positive things about being back here is that I'm home. I felt comfortable in the UK but I always knew it wasn't home. Here, I'm much more free – free to dress how I like, although when I go out in Dominica, I'm the odd one out because I don't dress Western, I dress African. I have been dressing like that for more than 30 years.

I have a beautiful home in Salisbury. There is no one around me. I can play my music; I don't have to consider the neighbours. In England, I could never have that lifestyle. Give Dominica it's due. I have three and a half acres of land. I sit on the veranda. I breathe fresh air. I get pumpkins, tomatoes, cucumbers from the soil. By me, it's heaven at the side of the mountain – the view is wonderful.

I'm a family person and the way of life here is more relaxed. My money can go further here. The education level is still good, and the level of crime is not high – I feel good about that. Since I've been back, I've been to nearly all the corners of the island – that's one wonderful thing. If I want to go to the hot-water springs, I go there; if I want to go to the sea, I go there. It's nice to be in your own place and you see your own people in positions of power.

I'm pleased I went to England – it changed me because going abroad gives you an open mind – over there life is completely different. But I am happy to be home; I am pleased to be here. But there are question marks and they leave me with asking that if I knew then what I know now would I make a choice and go somewhere else. If I was 10 years younger, I might go to Africa or Europe would call me; but taken all together I am happy to be home. ■

EUSTACE MAXIM

Eustace Maxim grew up in Layou Heights and went to London in 1960 as a young man to work and to give his family better opportunities. He and his wife returned in 2004 and live in Jimmit – he is involved in community work.

I was born in Grand Bay in 1937 but when I was four years old my parents moved to St Joseph. At that time people from the south and the east came to the west to work where the farms were more accessible. My parents were farm workers – they got a plot of land from an estate to work at Crown in the Layou Heights, and we lived there in rented accommodation, a farm building. We grew ground provisions, and then bananas came on the scene.

There were six children and to be honest we were very poor, although there was always food, and we were very happy. My parents couldn't afford to send me to school. One interesting thing is that when I was about eight we had a censor, and the chap got to our place and found us running around. And he said, "Where's your mother? Why you not at school?" And my mother came, and he said, "Make sure on Monday the children find themselves at school." Otherwise there would be a court summons. From then on, I had to go to school. But being from the country and being poor, maybe you go one week, and miss the next week. Perhaps you go for a few days, then miss a month, and so on. It wasn't constant. Our opportunities were very restricted.

Apart from working on the farm, at 15 or 16, I tried an apprenticeship as carpenter, but I had to go to town and I couldn't afford to stay there so I went back to my plantation. By the mid-1950s, banana was in so I found it easier to make a living.

The idea to go to England come about because I didn't have an education and I said to myself, well, if I'm going to have children, they're going to have better than I had. The opportunity in Dominica was very little. All my friends were moving away – to America, Canada, England. I felt I had to do something. People wanted better for their children and you couldn't get it in Dominica. Most people said they'd go for maybe five years to get a little money to start something back here. But it didn't turn out like that.

We knew something about the UK from what we read in books, nursery rhymes and things. And by the 1950s radio had just come on the scene so you could listen to the BBC. And we saw a few documentary newsreels at the cinema about England. But they almost always glamorise certain things so you don't see the real basics. Everyone had the idea that England was sweet looking. England was being talked about and you see someone who went before and come back and you see how their life style change. So you say, I'll give it a go. By and large we had a positive idea of England – in the colonial days it was drummed into your little head that it was the mother country. You see the grand come from the UK – they were the administrators, governors and what have you.

My aunt husband was there, and my auntie gave me his address. I sold my holding to a neighbouring farm to get the money for the boat and for pocket money. You bought the ticket at Whitchurch – the boats came every month and I left in April 1960.

The boat was very comfortable; they treat you very well. The food was good. You were going to the unknown but, fortunately, there were a couple of friends from St Joseph on the same boat. Our journey was about six weeks: we travelled south to Trinidad, then

Venezuela, and so on, there were many stops. Then to Italy, to France and Calais by train, a boat to Dover, then train to Victoria.

When I reached Victoria, it was afternoon, and I was expecting my aunt husband to meet me. But he didn't turn up. Everyone was meeting everyone, kissing and disappear. Unfortunately, I was waiting on the platform until I was the last one left. I wish the earth would open and swallow me up. So I thought, what must I do? I had a piece of paper with an address in East Ham. Luckily I had some money. I went to the taxi rank and told them where I was going, and they all said, no, no, no. They wouldn't give a reason. It came to my mind that it was because I was black.

We were told that if you're in England, the first thing you do is ask a policeman. So I asked a policeman. I said, "All the taxis are refusing to take me. What is the problem? Why will the taxis not take me?" And the policeman said, "At this time of the day they would rather go round the square mile." So I said, "Well, how do I get to this place?" So he said, "Go to the station and take a train to East Ham." I said, "How far is it?" He said, "In region of 10 miles."

Anyway, I went to the station, bought a ticket. One of the attendants showed me where to go. I went down the platform with a couple of suitcases on each arm; and found myself on the wrong side of the platform. Again, I used my initiative. I asked a porter, and show him the address and he told me it was the wrong platform. So I found the right platform but being green I didn't know anything – the train just run, stop, run, stop. When I realised the train had gone about 10 miles, I got off. But it was the wrong station. Funnily enough, the station I got off happened to be Barking, one stop from East Ham. Then I went to a taxi rank and there was no problem. It was a short trip round the corner. It was a very lonely experience and even now when I think of it I wonder how did I do it.

Well, I got to the address. My uncle was there. He was preparing his dinner. I was grateful he was there. He made me welcome. I stayed about a month until I could find a room. Those days work was plentiful – you could walk out of one job and into another. My uncle got me a job where he was working – they dismantled tractors, putting them in crates and sealed them for shipment. I stayed there for some time. Then I went to a place called Silvertown. There was a barge maintenance place there, on the River Thames. I worked there for a while. It was very hard work; it was mostly outdoors. You were always busy. Then I went to Standard Telephone and Cable, also in Silvertown, insulating telephone wires; I worked there quite a while. It was semi-skilled work operating a machine.

Apart from work, in those days, I wasn't into this pub thing, but there used to be a lot of house parties. That was the main source of entertainment. Well, I used to hear about teddy boys. You would hear that if you walk on the street you get beaten. I stayed away from the club scene – well, I had a wife back in Dominica and I didn't want to get involved. So I would meet a few friends from all over the West Indies – we had that one thing in common. Then you had company to walk back with. If you were alone you felt vulnerable. The only incident I can recall is that I was on my own once, and this group of lads – it was a wintry night, lots of snow – and they decide to throw snowballs.

I couldn't really save money – I was sending back to my wife, my mother and father. I had been married a month when I left. My wife was working in Dominica in the telephone company as an operator and she wasn't too keen on going to England. Then I came down for a visit in 1965 and I stayed for about six months. I tried to see if I could make a living here because she didn't want to leave. But I said there is nothing here for me. So I went back to England again.

London life: "In those days work was plentiful – you could walk out of one job and in to another."

'When you retire, now you can have the sunshine on your back, and you are having your reward for working so hard. You feel good about that.'

Jobs were still very much available – so when I get back I went to Ford's and worked there for quite a few years in the foundry until they close it down and take the plant off to Spain or somewhere. I took redundancy, and left to work in security – that job was very hard; mostly nights, long hours. Anyhow I stuck it out. Then my wife came when she got made redundant in 1969, and we got a two-roomed flat with all the amenities, in Forest Gate, and from there we get a council flat. It was important because you have all you the things you need under one roof, and the rent was reasonable. Going to England was always a means to an end for me. I work hard but I always thought that when I retire I wanted somewhere here to be comfortable.

All the time I sent money, there was an exchange of letters – and some agents in London that got newspapers from here, and I used to buy them. Then there was the association – I worked with DONA. I got involved since Hurricane David in 1979 – when the hurricane ravished the whole island, the call came out for help. So my wife and I thought we must do something. I went to buy saucepans, things like that, bags of rice. The reception point was 501 Harrow Road – it was the newly formed association. They said, whatever you have, take it. I thought I must join the association to keep in contact with Dominica and to have somewhere to go where we share the same ideas. I was very active in DONA.

My first trip back here after 1966 was in 1982 for a holiday, to see my family. My children were growing up – two was born in Dominica and two in the UK. That holiday made me want to come back – you look around and you see other people with the same intention, to buy a plot, to start building, and I really wanted to work towards that. When I came here that year, I opened a bank account. I had a brother-in-law here, who was very helpful. We had an allotment in St Joseph – but David blew the house away. There was nothing you could do about it. My wife didn't want to go back there so my brother-in-law found this lot in Jimmit. When we came here, we were one of the first people to move in.

My retirement was in 1998. So then we started making our preparations – we mostly used our money, but we had a loan from the credit union to supplement it, just so everything was in place. We didn't want to have to start and then stop. My stepdaughter, a school principal, and my brother-in-law looked after the building as it developed. We came in November 2004.

My experiences in the UK changed me a lot – I left here when I was 23 and most of what I know is from England. Except that when you're here, I used to like to be around people older then me – that's how you get experience. I find the young men they talk about how many children they father around the island and I keep saying I don't want to be in that kind of relationship. I have a wife and family and I want to be there for my children. You find the attitude of people who haven't travelled or gained experiences is so different. I can have a relationship with anyone now. What I find here is a lot of aggression, not exposed exactly, but I relate differently.

The best things about being in the UK were that it provided me with work. So I could work towards something – a future in Dominica. That was the main thing, and the worst thing that you have to bear is the cold. I have nothing bad to say about the UK. England gave me what I got. I appreciate it.

Back in Dominica, people don't realise that you go up there to better yourself, you work your butt off so to speak, and I find there's a lot of bickering, jealousy. When you retire, now you can have the sunshine on your back, and you are having your reward for working so hard. You feel good about that. The children are still in the UK but you only have to pick up the telephone or send emails. Most of my children make visits. My first son was born here; he likes it very much, and I think he's working towards his retirement here. We still have contact with England through DONA and our families.

Life here is peaceful. I feel comfortable. I try to get involved in associations and clubs in St Joseph. We do communal work – if someone wants to do something, and they cannot, we help them. We try to help people less fortunate than we are. We also have the Dominica Welfare and Hospital Aid Scheme – we help people who can't make their hospital bills – and I'm an active member. I would recommend Dominica to people – when you're at retirement age, it's the place to be. Where do you start to explain? There are so many places to go to – and wherever you are, you look around, and all you see is green. ■

BERNADETTE
AND LEONARD
ALEXANDER

Bernadette and Leonard Alexander were both born in Grand Bay. Leonard left in 1960 for England and Bernadette a year later. For many years Leonard made mannequins for Madame Tussauds' waxworks. They are now back in Grand Bay where they run the Campeche Guesthouse and Bar.

B*ernadette*: I was born in Grand Bay in 1943, but raised in Trafalgar – my mum is from Grand Bay but my dad was a farmer from Trafalgar. I would say I had a very happy childhood. We were free –we used to go swimming, play hopscotch, tell stories in the moonlight. Everyone had their chores – feeding the chickens and rabbits, collecting the eggs. My dad had his cows, and we had to take it in turns to take the milk to Roseau and come back in time for school. I spent a few years in Roseau where I lived with a lady named Mrs Harris – she used to take in young children to train to do different things. I made my first holy communion at her house. She used to show us how to do all kinds of things, how to make jam, tarts and cakes.

Leonard: When I was growing up in Grand Bay – I was born there in 1940 – it was a very good life, I can't complain. Everything was there for us – and there was 16 of us in the house. My parents worked hard to feed us. Mum had a bakery, and my father was a very good man, a farmer. I was enjoying going to school but I myself left at the age of 14 running away from a teacher – we changed classes and the new teacher didn't like me. From there, I went into tailoring. I learn well and I began to sew for people. How I was brought up was if you go out to work and make money everything has to go back to the house, you just leave it there for mummy.

Bernadette: We used to read our school books about England that London was the capital of the world, and like England was paved with gold but when we got there there was no gold.

Leonard: I never believed that England was paved with gold. Children saying that we must go to England to pick up gold, but when I arrive in England now, what am I picking up? Snow. At one time, they had a set of people from J Lyons in England who came around looking for people to go England to work, and sometime they pay the fare to go. They came to our house but my father was not there so they go away. I had two sewing machines and I was thinking whether to leave my machines and go to England. I would only spend five years and come back. I left in April 1960, and my father paid my fare. My parents were not so happy for me to go. When I was going my mum was crying, and the little ones were crying too. I said, "I will come back." When I arrived it was a bit dark, but I saw the red, white and blue flag. It was all horrible to speak the truth. I didn't like the fog, and sometimes I couldn't breathe. I only knew my sister and my brother in England. They met me at the station with Pam, a white friend of my sister, and they welcomed me. To speak the truth when I go to England I want to return here. But it was easier to leave here and go to England than to leave England and go here. It was so expensive.

Bernadette: In Dominica, work was scarce, and in Dominica to get a good job in the 1960s is who you know. You had to be the upper class to get a job; not with what's in your head or your qualifications, but that is how people got jobs here then. For people like me even though I would have the qualifications I didn't have the connections – that's the way it used to be, I wasn't Mr So and So's daughter.

I left, when I was 19, in September 1961 because everyone else was leaving, and looking for a better life. My dad paid my fare which

I had to work and send back. At the beginning I was excited because I am going to England, but when I get there I was a little bit disappointed. I got to Southampton and we got on the train for Victoria station. It was cold, horrible; I was a bit miserable, homesick. My sister and her now husband came to meet me and we went to Kentish Town in north London where we lived there until Leonard came along.

Leonard: I did know Bernadette from before – I met her in Roseau when I saw her passing on her bike. She was such a beautiful little girl, with a newspaper under her arm.

Bernadette: Not newspaper, a comic.

Leonard: In England, I was thinking of returning home but talking to a friend he said to me, "I have a nice cousin coming up here. As soon as she come, I'll come and get you." And when I went there I said, "Oh my god that's the girl I met in Roseau who was riding her little bike." So we talk and say hello, but she has a new boyfriend so she forgot all about this young man. That's how we met.

Bernadette: We got married six months after meeting. In those days, we used to go to other people's houses –mainly Dominicans, sometimes St Lucians. We didn't have much in those days but everybody was friendly, we mixed and enjoyed ourselves. Our intention was to stay five years and come back.

Leonard: I bring my passport in at the dole office, and one of them said, "You're in England for good you know." I said, "No way. Are you being serious?" He said, "You're going to stay here and work." I hear a lot of people complain about England but I can't – at work I was welcome.

Bernadette: My first job was in a cardboard box factory. I came as today; I had a rest the next day and the following day my sister took me to her workplace and I was hired straightaway.

Leonard: When I was first employed in the tailoring trade in England they gave me two half crown for the week. At the end of my first day, the man said, "You use the needle very well. Welcome for tomorrow morning." But the money in England was so small. I was better off in Dominica. So one day I walk from my home down to King's Cross, there was a job that was advertising for the town hall. So I walked up the road and saw some fellows sitting down outside, on their tea break. And one of them said, "Come here." So I turned back and he said: "I tell you to come here. Come here and I'll give you a job." I didn't know him and I walked inside into a huge factory. He was an Italian man and he said, "I'm going train you here and pay you well. You're a nice young man. Go home and come back at eight o'clock tomorrow morning and start to work." I didn't go for the other job again. My job was with Models London – we made mannequins for Madame Tussauds, and I worked there for 28 years. I did quite a lot of the big characters – Dr Kildare, Sony and Cher, General de Gaulle. The last big work we did was JR Ewing, and John Wayne.

Bernadette: The telephone wasn't popular in the early days so you would only write, and if you receive a letter and you'd go telling other people what happening. I did send money home, but it was a big sacrifice but it was expected of us. My first wages was £1.10s a week. At that time a lot of West Indians in England used to save with the "sub". Say there were 10 people, and everybody put in say £5 every week and when you get to £100 someone take that money. The person that's in charge takes your name, and decides who needs the money most so that person will take it first. Then those who need it next and so on. That's how people saved their money at the beginning. It was a long time before we start to come back to visit. The money wasn't there. Leonard went first in 1974 when they had the big riot in Grand Bay.

Leonard: To tell the truth I was saying to myself the only thing that will bring me back to Dominica is my mother and my father. I say my prayer but I was so terrified – the guns, the cutlass, the knives. A group of fellas smoking pipes, they call themselves Rastafarians. They were friendly but they were scary. When I left here and went to England there was no such thing called "Dreads". What we had were well-dressed young men and polite. Every weekend we would take a walk to Petit Savanne – we respect one another. But when I came here in 1974, I said to mummy, "This place no good." I couldn't believe that was Grand Bay.

Bernadette: In England, we were part of the Grand Bay UK Community Alliance and also DUKA for a while. The best thing of living in England you could go to Europe, you could take the coach for the weekend, and go on the ferry. We had our little going away bag and whenever the Alliance was doing a trip, we're off.

Leonard: I was the welfare officer for the Alliance. I visited people in hospital and we did fund-raising to send to this village. We sent down two concrete mixers and two lawn mowers for the playing field.

Bernadette: We sent cricket bats and books for the library, and computers for the schools.

Leonard: No one ever said thank you to us. Nobody. The last gift we gave we raised EC$17,000. If you go to the playing field, go in the bar, and check out the fridge and freezer, we provide that.

Bernadette: By the early 1970s, we all wanted to go back to Dominica, we were homesick so we settled here for a year. We sold our house in London, packed up and came down with our two kids – they went to school here – and at that time there was a small wooden house for us. We broke it down and built something concrete. We spent a lot of money building so we had to go back to work in England and people said we were too young to be in Dominica.

Leonard:
'They just think because you go to England you pick up money on the ground. They don't appreciate how hard we had to work for it.'

Leonard: I left my job at Madame Tussauds. I wanted my two boys to know here properly and give them a bit of experience in school here. I told my boss that I would come back and not to give my job to anybody. You could always go back; work was always there, and I went back to London after a year. And when we heard about Hurricane David in 1979, I came down the day after. When I reach Grand Bay, my home was flat down, mummy's home was flat down. They were at my brother's home, but they couldn't believe I made it to Grand Bay. I helped quite a few people.

Bernadette: When I came back later with the last boy, Jeremy, we spent six years here. I came back with him because some of the schools were terrible in England. I didn't think the children were being taught properly. It was a tough decision. The other two boys could take care of themselves by then. Jeremy went to Roseau Grammar School and he reckons he's a true Dominican. Then I fell ill and I had to go to London to have an emergency operation, and poor Jeremy had to stay here and do his own cooking and washing and go to school. That was a strain on him. My sisters used to come up and keep an eye on him. I stayed nine months in England, and then I came down and took him up – he had graduated from the grammar school.

Leonard: In London, we sit down and discuss about building this place. I bought that ground from the government years ago. From childhood I used to play here and I used to say maybe one day I'll have a piece of land here that belongs to me and this thinking it worked. I did it, I bought the land and we built Campeche Guesthouse and Bar.

Bernadette: When he had a few bob he just get up and go. He asked me, "Are you coming?" that was before the place was built, and I said, "No, I'm getting good lolly. Give me six months." He came on his own, and I finally came down in May 2006. We were retired by then. My sons can look after themselves but I have a granddaughter and a grandson and that was very very hard to leave them behind.

Leonard: She was in England when I was here supervising the building work. We had a tough time with the builder.

Bernadette: They want to do what they want to do. They should do what you want them to do.

Leonard: I said, "If you're not doing what I want you to do, leave it and go."

Bernadette: When you come home, we respect everybody, but in return most of the people don't respect us. We give them work... It's give, give, give, all the time, and all the time they want to take, take, take. It's jealousy and greed. What we worked for overseas for 30 or 40 years, right, so we sell our house and get a bit of money. We come down here to do something. What we've worked so hard for so many years, they want to take it in a year. They want all of it. That's the way I feel. You ask them to do something they charge you an arm and a leg, two, three times more than they would charge somebody else.

Leonard: Some of our people here, they're not very nice. You give them work, you give them drink, you give them food but they have an attitude. We're Dominicans, but their attitude is that we shouldn't be here, we're foreigners. They've got to stop that. They just think because you go to England you pick up money on the ground. They don't appreciate how hard we had to work for it, but I don't discuss things with those people.

> Bernadette:
> 'If we had abandoned Dominica
> we wouldn't be here at all,
> would we? If you come from
> England, they sideline you.'

Bernadette: People in Grand Bay will say hello, but if you're doing something and you think they'll come and support you they don't. They're only for those who have not left the island. They say that we do things here, like the bar, for people from England. That is not true, but they don't see it that way. Some Dominicans say that returnees have a superior attitude but if we see things are going wrong, things are not right, it's a free country we have to speak out. That's not the same as having a superior attitude.

Leonard: We're Dominicans. If things are wrong we have to say this is wrong.

Bernadette: Or they say that those who left abandoned Dominica. Those who left Dominica and didn't come back it's different, but if you leave Dominica and keep coming back all the time, how can we abandon our country. If we had abandoned Dominica we wouldn't be here at all would we? If you come from England, they sideline you. It's the attitude of the people here – they think you shouldn't come. Because we're getting a regular pension they don't like it.

Leonard: The other thing is our government urging people when they are overseas to come home but when you are home people change; they don't care about you anymore.

Bernadette: For instance at the customs when you bring your stuff the amount of money that they charge you might as well leave it behind. They say they give you duty free but I don't call that duty free.

Leonard: To speak the truth, I wouldn't tell anybody to come home. I used to tell everyone, let's go home but now we think twice. There needs to be something to bring people together and talk to people. They don't understand. There needs to be some kind of discussion. If all the returnees get together and have a general meeting and invite people, like the prime minister and others, to come to ask questions. That could be done.

Bernadette: For someone coming I would say be prepared – because it's going to be a rough ride until you're settled down. And if I had to think everything again I would take my savings and go on a cruise, go on holiday and don't build this place at all. It's dragging, it's boring, there's nothing to keep you active and lively. You can get a couple of people to stay, then you do the cooking and you feel you are alive, you know. But there are changes for the good. There's some development, there's the nice playing field to play football, cricket, what have you. There's a lot of building being put up by people coming from overseas and from the village themselves. I'm glad to be back although it's been a rough ride and I miss my sons and grandchildren. We have a little group for us returnees and other people too, from Grand Bay. Whoever want to join are welcome. We have things like barbecues and then we socialise. But things are a bit quiet now.

Leonard: I'm pleased to return home to say the truth. The nicest thing is you are free – if I want to have a walk I just go. You can relax in your house and go and have a swim. What we have here in Dominica I appreciate it very very much. But sometimes I watch kids eating two mangoes and there's nothing in the house to eat. There's a lot of poverty here. I'm happy to be back but when I was a small boy before I went to England I was happy. Now I am happy and am glad to be here although I miss my sons. ■

NURSIE FREDERICK

Nursie Frederick was raised in Salisbury and went to England when she was 17 to get married. She had two children and worked in nursing until taking early retirement. She and her husband returned in 1998 and live in Mero.

I took just a little brown suitcase with me to England, with a few little cotton dresses, little thin things, no cardigan, no jumper. I was 17 and knew nothing about England – all I knew was that I had three brothers and a sister there and I was going to get married. My brothers wrote to me but they didn't really explain about the country. All we knew was that it was cold. But apart from that I hadn't got a clue. My initial thought was to stay five years but I ended up staying nearly 40 years.

I was born in 1943 and raised in Salisbury. My dad was the sexton of the Salisbury catholic church and my mum was a seamstress and used to help out at the presbytery. There were nine of us – five girls and four boys. My eldest brother emigrated with my aunt to British Guiana and I never saw him again. My second brother went to St Mary's Academy, and I passed my exams to the Convent but my parents couldn't afford to send me, so after I left Salisbury government school I went to the Convent industrial school, with the nuns, making mats and bags.

It was a good childhood, and I had lovely, understanding parents. We were not rich but we managed. Our food portions were quite small, but we were satisfied. In those days, what we had put on our plate, it fills you up; God looks after his children. Our school was

95

right on the beach and when we had our break we had a quick swim and if the teacher noticed we were wet, we were in trouble. After school we had to rush home for our "afternoon". We had a glass of lime squash and half of a penny bread. Looking back it's so nice.

I worked for a year, and then this young man from Salisbury wrote me and asked me to join him in England. I knew him before – he went to the same church and school – he was talking to me but I didn't believe. I gave my mother the letter and she said he had to write to my parents and my parents wrote back to him and agreed.

The day I left was a Tuesday, August 2nd 1960. We travelled on the boat for three weeks and landed first in Genoa, and then took the train to Victoria Station. I enjoyed the journey and I had relatives travelling the same day as well. I was well protected.

My two brothers and my husband-to-be, Mr Frederick, met me at Victoria station – this big place, you felt like a little thing in a big globe. The terraced houses all had chimneys and there was smoke coming out of each chimney in those days. I thought the chimneys were bakers' ovens – and that they're baking their breads in their homes. My husband-to-be was staying in Southall, in west London, and we had one room in the house of his sister. My brothers and most of my other relatives were not too far away. The people were very prejudiced. You got those dirty looks but you try not to take any notice of them because you are here for a reason.

I arrived on August 18 and started work the next Monday – my brother had found me a job doing assembly work in Magnatex, a car components factory. It was a big difference to my work in Roseau, but you just fit yourself in. I was earning £4 and 6s a week. You know you had to earn to buy your food, pay your rent and I had to buy my clothes for winter. My first winter was horrible. In the house where we lived, the toilet was outside – oh my God, and when you sat on the

In London in the 1970s.

'Those who come anticipating their life will be just like England it can never ever be. If you come down here and you still want to keep eating baked beans and all that. No ... You have to come with a mind that you make do with what you can get.'

seat it was freezing cold; in the 1960s we suffered, you know.

I kept in touch with my family – but I didn't tell them things that might make them feel sad. If they're not there to experience it they might worry so you try not to tell them in too much detail. It was part of the objective to send money to my family. My dad was earning not very much so I regularly sent money home, and at Christmas and Easter it was a must. I missed the heat, the sunshine, and my family. But after a while you settle down, do your best, spend some and save some, and in 1962 we bought our own house.

We lived among our people – mostly Salisbury people. So we didn't go out and socialise until my brother formed his own band and he used to keep dances at the community centre on feast days. It was all Caribbean people, not English and it was all black people's music. It was good fun. Dominicans had an association in Southall where they had dances every now and again.

The only time I didn't work was when I had the children. When I had my son I went back to work when he was three months old. I had a white nanny who left him in his pram all day; the back of his head had gone all bald. You could tell she wasn't taking him much out of his pram. Don't forget I am a young person, I didn't know much about babies. I'm just learning. But the Almighty Lord, he took care of that. Then, my daughter was born in Dominica because I had come in 1966 when my mum wasn't well. We stayed for just over a year. I was glad to be out of the cold. We tried to teach the children the patois – they picked some up. It's a good second language for them, they know a few words but not much. I talked to them about their grandparents and they enjoyed it when they came.

I worked for Hoovers from 1972, and when I was made redundant in 1981, I joined the nursing profession working as a nursing auxiliary. I stayed there in St Bernard's psychiatric hospital and then upgraded to the health centre in Greenford at a higher salary. Altogether I worked in nursing nearly 17 years and then retired. I never intended to retire in England. I was in the bus one morning on my way to work and I saw an old woman, it was about ten to seven, running to catch the bus. And I said, please God, don't let that ever happen to me – a little old lady, all her hair was grey, running to catch the bus at that time in the morning. And I thought retirement in England must be boring – because you're locked up in the house all day and if you go out you have to go out into the cold.

But when you get over there at first, you don't think of coming back too soon and in those days the travelling was much more difficult and the finance – you'd have to come by boat and that took three weeks. My husband was the one who really wanted to come back. He came here for a visit in 1985 and when he came back he said, "Nursie, I've bought a piece of land." I said, "What! You bought land. When are you going back to Dominica?" We'd never talked about that but I suppose he had it in his mind. At that time I didn't have any intention of coming home, I was quite happy in England.

My husband came down to Mero to start building in 1990 and my husband sister looked after it. We build the whole of the upstairs. I had an uncle who lived in Mero – so I am the one to follow in his footsteps. Salisbury was so congested that I didn't want to live there. The scenery over the sea here is beautiful. Mero is the biggest beach in Dominica and they're really promoting it. It's really nice.

We sold our house in England and we both took early retirement – we were lucky to get that – in November 1998, and as soon as we retired we moved down. We brought everything down in a container, including our vehicle. The hardest thing was leaving my children and two beautiful grandchildren. It was sad for the children – and my grandchildren, they're the ones I miss. But from 2000 – for seven consecutive years – I find that I have the opportunity of going back to England because my son is an aircraft engineer so I used to get staff travel. So I cannot grumble.

I am glad to be back, and especially my husband – he wanted to come back for his parents. Although now they have passed away, he was happy to spend time with his parents. When we first came, to get things in town was like a hazard. Everything was slow, slow. When you have problems it's a job to find someone to fix it. My biggest job is cleaning inside the house because it's the same level with the road. These are my only hassles. Apart from that I'm quite happy.

I'm a Catholic, and in England I went to St Anselm's, Southall – that's where I got married. But when you work in the nursing profession you work shifts and there were many, many Sundays I didn't go to church because I had go to work– so circumstances were different. Now it's paying back time to the Lord and I am thanking

With her daughter, Karen, as a
baby, and son Derek in 1967.
"The hardest thing about
leaving England was leaving my
children and two beautiful
grandchildren."

him for the many graces he's given to me and my family. Three nights
in the week I go to church in the evening and on Sunday mornings.
Then Tuesday morning, I go to six o'clock mass. That is my main
thing for the week.

I also go swimming. I've got a very good friend in Pointe Michel
and we go for a swim. She is a Dominican, and is the only one who
gets my husband to the sea. I have a sister in Salisbury – she's the
one who looked after my mum the most so I feel I need to look after
her myself; and one in St Joseph – she's a returnee like me. Otherwise
we don't have any socialising with other people at the moment.

I know that I come from Dominica – I know it's my country. I love
my country dearly, no one is coming to push me around, from
England or nowhere else. They call us English – especially my
husband. I don't mind that. I'm a Dominican and if you choose to call

me English that's up to you. At first it was tough but now you're settling in your home and everything is in place.

I have never felt rejected here – this is my country. Those who come anticipating their life will be just like England it can never ever be. If you come down here and you still want to keep eating baked beans and all that. No. The life is so different, everything's different from England – you have to come with a mind that you make do with what you can get. But in England you buy what you want but you can't do that in Dominica. You mustn't, how would I put it, show off on the people. You know where you came from, you know what life was about. Instead of doing that, talk to them, help them out. They think you showing off on them so they retaliate so to speak.

And sometimes you have to help the people here as well. But, oh my God, our people are so different here now. If they come to your place, you give them a piece of food, they say, "Go, put it in a container. I'll bring it for you." They never do. You never see that container. They say, "Lend me a spanner." You never see that spanner.

I think that those who feel they want to come back, the more the merrier because it will build the country. But I don't think Dominica is ready for young people. Young people are better off left up there. I wouldn't advise my children to come here. My daughter is a manager in a big company; my son is an aircraft engineer. I wouldn't advise them to come here and even if they get that job here the salary is next to nothing.

The best thing about being in Dominica is the warmth, and being back in my own country. And I'm thanking the Almighty Lord for looking after me all those years in England and keeping me safe there – for nearly 40 years. ■

MICHAEL BARON

Michael Baron is a Carib from Bataca. He left in 1960 as a young man for England. He worked mainly as a chef and looked after his three children when his first wife died. He returned in 2007 with his second wife and lives in Antrizle.

The first man who gave me the idea to go abroad was the owner of a house where I stay when I was working on the roads in Marigot. Every afternoon the other workers went in the bar, and he said to me, "You don't belong here." I was a Carib boy, shy, I always stay apart. He said, "Look round you – everybody drinking, smoking, playing dominoes – you don't belong here. Go away, go to England."

There were two Caribs who go to England before I went and they went in the 1950s – but they couldn't make it and they came back. They said it was cold, it was hard to get accommodation and they just couldn't cope. But I just feel yes, this man is right and it stick in my head. But when I told my mother and stepfather, he went up the roof. My stepfather said, "You cannot go. You are the only one who is helping me." So I became very unhappy, and my mother noticed I was changed – not jolly as I used to be. She said to me that if I was going to be unhappy she's not the one who is going to make me unhappy. So I will go. So then my uncle wanted to go and my mother said to him, "I'll give you the money. You go, work, send back the money," and then he would send for me and I would have a place to go. When he wrote, the thought of going there became stronger because he said he was earning so much money per week and I thought most people doesn't earn that a year here. This is where I read it wrong – because he never said about having to pay rent, heating bill, bus fares and so on. But I said to myself, I can only spend two years there, then come back and build my house, buy a car, work my farm and I'll be fine.

I was born at Bataca in the Carib Territory in 1940. My mother was 100 per cent Carib – everybody had respect for her – and my father, who died when I was about eight, had link with Caribs but he come from Petite Savanne. My mother struggled to bring us up – there were people round you who really love you and what you don't have it's because they cannot give it to you. Growing up was good but it was hard. We was not educated. My aim was to work the land because that's how you put food on the table. I only go to school very very few days a month – the nearest school was in Salybia and it was a long way to go.

I would spend my Sundays at Antrizle beach after church. We swim and we have competition dive, we go down and pick sand until our eyes is all bloodshot. I used to play cricket, dominoes and go fishing on the rock at night in the river with the other Carib boys. My mother used to tell us about the Carib myths and this big rock here – the Pagua Rock – they say, during evolution, four animals or insects come out from the sea, one come up here and that rock is his house up there. And at Sineku, they say that the snake come out of the sea, and then the centipede trail where the pattern in the rock they say it was a giant centipede. I was told them but I never really believe that sort of thing. My mother didn't do any craft; my mother was in the forest, the mountain, the garden – she was the man. My grandfather used to be telling me about the herbs. Doesn't matter what kind of illness you had, he would go and get the bush and crush it or bath you with it or make you drink it and you will get better. In those days, when the Caribs go to Marigot or Wesley, they want to call them

Injun – they are always nagging them. Before I see it a lot, but it's changed and now I haven't seen the Caribs ill-treated.

They built a school in Atkinson so when I was about 12 or 13 I started going to school. Because I miss so much school they had to put me in the lowest class but then the teacher made me his messenger boy to run errands for him even on examination day. He did that to me for three years and I was stuck in that class but my mother could not do anything because at that time women had no voice. I told my mother I cannot go back so my stepfather put me to work. We went in the bush – we used to spend a whole week there – and I did that for about two years. And then I got a little job, at Marigot with a man who was cleaning the roads and so on. And then when I was 20, I went to England. My mother was scared for me but she knew that my ambition was strong. I went in September 1960. We send my uncle all the details of me coming and I got his address and I went. I was excited but I was scared because I get sea-sick, and I was sick for 16 days.

Nobody met me in Victoria station – my uncle didn't turn up. I have the address but I have no money – and he didn't live in London but in the country. There were two chaps from Delices who come on the same boat – and one of them we share the same cabin, and his auntie came to pick them up. And she said, "Who come to meet you?" When I told her, she said, "We can't leave you here." I am shivering, I'm hungry and cold. This is a lady who touched my heart – I always say she saved my life. At that time, the place is dark, cold, people wasn't friendly and I don't know where I'm going. So the lady take me home, me and my friend we throw mattress on the floor and we make ourselves comfortable.

The third day I was in London, I went to the Cumberland Hotel in Marble Arch and get a job as a kitchen porter. And the lady said to me, "When you get your wages I'm coming shopping with you. You need warm clothes." I had a suitcase with just short-sleeve sport shirt and underpant and a couple of trousers, that all I had, nothing else. The lady went to do shopping with me and buy a nice woolly jumper.

After about a month I tell her I must look for my own room. It was very hard to find accommodation. You could see, "Room to Let – no blacks, no Irish, no dogs." I saw that with my own eyes. There used to be teddy boys and they used to walk down the road in the evening and beat up black people. This was the big threat in England. One day they threaten me and said, "We'll catch you tomorrow night." They knew where I work, I was worried sick – they used to kill people. So I took a carving knife, and wrapped it in newspaper. I see them coming, four of them, and one of them had a bicycle chain and they're looking at me as if to say, "You're meat today." Then I pulled the carving knife – and said, "If you willing to die, I am willing to die." And they stood and I crossed the road. They never trouble me again.

The kitchen I work in all the menu is in French. I speak patois so I always understand it. I always make sure I have clean clothes and I finish my work quick and go to serve in the restaurant. So one day they give me a job as a chef – and I thought I can handle that. You don't give in – I work hard and I do it good. I work there for four years – and then I went to work for a Berni Inn in Uxbridge where it was mostly grilling. I earned £20 a week but it was much harder because I have to do split duty, and I cannot go home in the afternoon, and I finish at eleven. I work like that for more than two years.

In England, I never even pass as a West Indian. And even now very few people know about Carib people. Every other people think I was Portuguese or Puerto Rican. People didn't know how to treat me, I wasn't black I wasn't white. Once I was sitting having a bowl of soup and two Dominicans came and sat next to me. They were talking patois and one said, "*Ca ka fet*?" thinking I wouldn't understand. I said, "*Mwen bien. Ca kont ou*?" They didn't know what to say – their mouths were wide open. Even though they knew about Caribs, they thought I was Portuguese or Spanish.

When I got to England I wrote back to my mum and I begin to pay her back the money for my fare, but six month later my mother die, she was 40. She had an operation but she decided to go back to work too quick – and the stitches burst inside. Because the blood formed a mass inside her – so people said people make obeah on her. I heard about it by letter but the worst was I cannot come back. Not enough money. I feel so bad – I thought after all her hard work and allowing me to go to England, I don't think I thanked her enough. In the end I get over it but it was a very very hard time.

Always I had the plan to come back. I know I could make it in Dominica with hard work and I went up there to make it happen quicker. Dominica was always on my mind. The first thing I told my first wife – she was from southern Ireland – was that I have to go back. I kept in contact with my sister. I am very close to her and every Christmas I send her £25 even when things were hard. When things were really bad I didn't write her. I didn't want to tell her my problems, what can she do? I didn't want her to feel sorry for me.

I had three children with my first wife but she died when she was 38 from a thrombosis. When she died – the children were six, 11 and 13. I did not have not a single soul to help me. By then I had moved to Slough and I was working at Wexham Park hospital as the night cook, and somebody report me that I left the children on their own. So one day I reach home and I didn't have my children. It was a few weeks after my wife die. I nearly went crazy. They never let me know – they just came, got the police and ejected my children. And never even notified me. I found out somehow where they were. I thought I would kill someone – I was so angry. I went to court. That's the only way I could get them back. The court told me that if you give up your job you can have your children back. So I had to give up my job and I'm having my three children going to school, rent to pay. So things getting bad again.

In England I try help my community back in Dominica. I was a member of the Dominica Carib Association who help building the hospital in the Carib Reserve, and after Hurricane David I help raise funds for Atkinson and Salybia schools and also the school in Petite Savanne to send new text books. I also brought two brothers from Antrizle to England and gave them a home and found them work.

The first time I came back was in 1988 with my elder son – it was 28 years after I left. I was very very pleased and all my children were happy for me – my other son and daughter were celebrating for me because they knew I wanted to come back so much. I came for two months and stayed with my sister in Bataca. Later my sister came and spent six months in England. That time my sister realised how hard it was when she saw the amount of snow coming down. Up to now, my sister can say that it is not an easy life in England.

The first day we arrive – it rained for five days non-stop. My son couldn't believe so much rain. He love it – the only non-Dominican son that come to Dominica and eat everything they put in his plate. He get up one morning and said I'm going to get this rooster that woke me up. He get a portion of bread and a glass of rum and soak bread in the rum and feed the chicken and hold the chicken and chop his head off. And they show him how to pluck it. And they cook it, and he eat. I think he would be more rooted to the Carib if we did take him on more holidays, but he went back and take the English way again. But he remember my sister and what he did in Dominica.

When I was bringing up the kids I do a variety of part-time jobs

> ‘When I came back I remember I was walking to the beach and just had my camcorder and I videoed the hummingbird suckle and I thought isn't that nice – before I took all that for granted. And I said to myself this is my paradise jungle. I love it. ’

but all the time my plan is to have the money to come down and build my house. All my life – I don't think I could die happy if I didn't come down. But when you buy a house in England you don't have any more saving – all the money went on the mortgage. I became very ill during that time – I had a pain in my chest, and every time it take me, it last longer. So I said to myself I have to die in Dominica, not in England. I said I would have to sell the house but it was the 1990s and the recession. Every month the price went down and down but I determined to come back.

So when at last I sold my house in England, I come down in 1996, and I want to buy this land and the house of my stepfather. I look at it – it's a brick house – and I thought there wouldn't be much wrong with it but it wasn't like that. The house was cracked in the middle and no one would climb on the roof to repair it. But I renovated it and stayed for two and a half years. During that time I became very healthy – all the pains went. I work hard. I carry bucket of sand, concrete – helping with the house. I thought, if I'm going to die I'm going to die happy.

It take me a little while to settle back. I didn't know the people – they looking me like stranger. But the old people tell them, he live here before, he is one of the Baron boys. After a while I begin to have friends – it was good. Before I went back to England it was so good –

"The best thing about coming back home is my health. When I'm in Dominica I can move my shoulder ... I pick my jelly coconut, dig my dasheen and my tannia."

I could make jokes with them if I'm there having a drink in the shop.

They accepted me back but there's always a thing in the Carib Territory that they think they have authority for everything in the Carib Territoy – that they have a right for it. But I change so much – this is mine, if you want it you have to ask. I plant coconuts – they used to steal it and think that it's theirs. That's one reason why I can't build my house there and why I now live in Antrizle. I still have a portion of land in Bataca but I cannot stay there because of the attitude of some of the young – they drink, they smoke drugs, they have no respect. The way I was brought up and grow up in England again, I just need peace and quiet.

Then I had to go back to England because I had no money left – I'd spent the money renovating. So I got a job with BT O2 as a cleaning supervisor – that is where I met my wife Annette. She came to Dominica, and she like it but she have a close family in England – I know how hard it is for her. We came back for good in 2007. Now I will go back to England only when I have to. I spent two and half month there and I was miserable and Annette said, "I can't bear to see you miserable." She know I cannot stay in England. She is a very very loving person – she has a real heart, and she understands.

The best thing about coming back home is my health. When I'm in Dominica I can move my shoulder – I pick my jelly coconut, dig my dasheen and my tannia. I can go in the sea and get a good soaking, and sit in my shed and do my woodwork, when I want and when I feel. And that is so good. In England, I cannot go outside – I'm bored inside.

I could say it was a very good experience to go to England because if I never see it with my own eye I don't think I would believe what people tell me. I had a hard time and a reasonable time but I never give up. In all fairness I'm still alive; I can still work and move about, and I don't think England do me really really good but it didn't do me too bad either. I would tell any Dominican to come back – for your own benefit and also so you can help others. I can see many people doing foolish things and I can see a lot of people who have been abroad have the knowledge, even if it's just to talk about it, to try and change things.

When I was a boy in Dominica, I didn't appreciate Dominica because I was working like a man. When I came back I remember I was walking to the beach and had my camcorder and I videoed the hummingbird suckle and I thought isn't that nice – before I took all that for granted. I said to myself, this is my paradise jungle. I love it. And I write on the beach, "This is Baron beach." I was very, very happy. ■

VISAS

SYLVESTER JOSEPH

No.
Landed in the Colony
Section 12 (1)
Condition 2 days
Date 11/10/60

Sylvester Joseph went to London at 17 in 1960. He worked in the Post Office for many years. He was also the first chairman of the Dominica UK Association. He returned in 1984 and became a prison officer. He now lives in Fond Melle.

I left Dominica in 1960 when I was 17 and my first visit back was in 1977 and to be honest that blew my mind. I had become a bit disenchanted with life in England, I didn't see me growing old there – one of the things I noticed was that working among English people is that their life revolved around work, their football team and the pub. They would retire, we would have a collection for them and a farewell do, then six months or so later, we'd have a collection for the widow. Why work all that long time to retire and then within a short space of time you are history? I put it down to the life style – they were so involved in work and football and when you took one thing out of it there was nothing left and they passed on to the great yonder. I didn't want that for myself, I wanted a long retirement. And then when I came down to Dominica I saw for myself how my school friends were enjoying life. I thought I am missing something. They had a better life than I did, and I am just surviving so I had better come back down and get a piece of the action. That is what motivated me and from that time all I could think about was, I'm going home, I'm going home, I'm going home.

Dominica has always been a migrating society. Even from the time of slavery it was exporting slaves to other islands, and, essentially, we have continued to export people up until this day. I was born in

Aruba where my father was working in the oil industry and came back to Dominica when I was one. I lived in Roseau with my mother but she is from Riviere Cyrique and that's where I claim as home.

My childhood was OK. It wasn't easy for my mother. It was not a luxurious life to be honest, and when kids from better off families were getting presents and new clothes, I had to make do. I was my mother's only child but she helped to raise a cousin of mine, so there were two of us. After my mother left for the UK I went to live with two of my aunts in Roseau. At first I went to private schools – my mother was hung up on education; she had been a teacher – then I went to Roseau Mixed School and then to the Dominica Grammar School.

There we had a very classical English education – we even had to do Latin. It was almost a public-school education. There was very little about the Caribbean in our education – it was the usual Rule Britannia thing. The heroes were English heroes – John Hawkins, Walter Raleigh, and our literature was essentially English, all the classics. If there was any West Indian history it was written from a British point of view, not from a black man's perspective. We picked up stuff on the Haitian revolution but a lot of that was from our own reading. Only later one read CLR James and Frantz Fanon, and then you got an understanding from our own perspective.

My mother left for England when I was 13. They were leaving then by the boatloads, up until I left myself. Everybody felt the mother country was where it was at. For me, going to England was a matter of no choice – your mother says you have to come up, so you have to come up. My mother thought it would be better for me to come up to England and start working. She wrote to say she was working and stuff like that but there was no detailed explanation of life in England. I just had to come and find out for myself. Like everybody else who was leaving Dominica, one said, look, I'm going up for five years and at the utmost 10. It was just a temporary thing and we'll be back shortly. There was no real sadness. It was something one took in one's stride. It was exciting that it was something new, to go up to see things we had read in books.

To catch the boat – it was called the *Franca* "C" – I had to go to St Lucia by schooner. It was very rough and with the smell of copra in an enclosed space it was not a pleasant trip. It was a nine-day journey to England – there were only four of us who had travelled from Dominica – and it took me quite a few days to get accustomed. I think I didn't eat for about five days: the seas were rough and the food was a totally new experience for me. The smell was entirely different to anything I'd known. We landed at Genoa and had to take a train across Europe to Calais and then the boat to Dover and from there by train to Victoria.

When I landed at Dover and then going through the countryside, I thought it was rather dismal – it was dark, so grey, almost lifeless, in complete contrast to what I had been accustomed to. It was an anti-climax: one had visions of colour, ceremony and pageantry and acres of green and castles, and all you saw was grey. At the time it was late autumn so fog was the order of the day.

We lived in Poplar, east London, just off East India Dock Road. It was the heart of Cockney land – there were white people around, but the house we lived in was a multi-storey building with two sets of Grenadians, a family from British Guiana, a gentleman from Barbados and one from Jamaica. At the time people only had rooms available to them; one didn't have houses and flats as people do now. When I lived in Dominica, with one aunt, I shared a room with my cousins, but with my other aunt I had my own room. There in England, it was cramped: I had to share a biggish room with my mother and her husband – the only thing separating us was a curtain.

Within a couple of days I had to go down to register to get a National Insurance number, and then go to the employment bureau. I ended up working in a lumber mill on the Mile End Road. It was winter and you had to climb stacks of cut lumber, sometimes covered with snow. So it wasn't particularly easy but you didn't have the choice. I didn't suffer from chilblains – one of the things everyone complained about. Initially the weather wasn't so much of a problem; I only began to have a problem with the cold when I became older.

Within a year I applied to what was then the General Post Office. I got a job behind the counter – and that gave me an opportunity to meet a very wide cross-section of people both behind the counter and the people who I served. I did enjoy it – I had moments of fun.

Very early on, when I went to work for the Post Office, I joined the union. My mother had worked as a typist at the Dominica Trade Union office so in a way I was brought up in that movement. West Indians generally are very much into the union thing, especially those of us who had grown up in the Caribbean. I began playing an active role quite early on and at one time I got to be assistant branch secretary and treasurer of the branch. I attended conference, attended workshops, and I played a part in the big Post Office strike in the late 1960s.

In the end I have to say I fell out with the union because I saw it as my role to represent all the membership. The Post Office had a rule that you could not take your vacation during the Christmas period. But a number of us from the Caribbean would like to visit back home and the most popular time was around Christmas – and that was also true for the Irish and even the English who had relatives in Australia and New Zealand. So I said if the Post Office could be persuaded to allow persons to accumulate their leave, even

"We had a very classical English education – we even had to learn Latin. There was very little about the Caribbean in our education – it was the usual Rule Britannia thing."

if it was only once in every five or 10 years, it would afford them the opportunity to visit family and friends. But the union were the ones to object to it, and I thought their job was to represent me. Their objection was that it was only black people who were going to benefit; and I thought that smelled very much of racism, and I felt I could not be part of a movement that was racist. So I left the union.

I didn't really meet up with overt racism although there were people along the way who had racist tendencies. Even quite early on, when a number of us went to night school, we fought street battles with young whites because of racial differences, but I did not let that affect my thinking in terms as to how I related to society. But there was racism without a doubt, and one place I did experience racism was at church. Three of us went to church – to a Catholic church in Poplar – every Sunday morning, and when mass was over the priest went outside and shook hands with his congregation. Sunday after Sunday we would stand around waiting for a handshake, and that never ever came. At that time we were the only blacks going to that church, and he shook hands with every one else but us. One winter I thought to myself, why are you waking up every Sunday, snow or shine, to go to church and you are not welcome? It does not make sense. So I thought that's it, finished, I'm not going back. I took that very personal – I was extremely disappointed. If there was one place that I expected a welcome it was a church, and it was not there.

Instead, and it was almost like going to church, you would go down to Hyde Park Corner and listen to the speakers there – you had the Black Power movement and the freedom for Africa movement – and when there were demonstrations one joined that. The whole thing about going to Hyde Park became my Sunday activity and I also used to enjoy walking in the City of London. At that time, in the 1960s, on Sundays, it was almost a graveyard. It was quite beautiful – one walked through historical streets and lanes, and you could almost feel the persons who had walked those streets in history being around. That was how I would while away my hours. In a way I am a solitary person – I enjoy company but I also enjoy quiet, and for me at that time the City was just the place for me. My closest friends were from other islands, and then at one time we went clubbing together – it was like a six-day a week thing: dancing at the Q club, the Flamingo, mostly West End clubs.

It was still on my mind to go back home, particularly at Christmas time that was the worst, worst, worst period. There were no vehicles going around – and very few of us had transport – and you were stuck in the house. You just sat there and looked out of the window to see the snow falling. You felt, if I was in Dominica I would be doing this and doing that. At that time, it was rather lonesome.

One of the reasons people did not go home after the five years was that some of the things we thought we were going to do, like study, didn't happen. In the UK it was practically impossible to work and study – it has to be full time – and even night school is a bit of a problem. At the end of your working day you cannot go to night school – you're so tired, you cannot perform. I had originally wanted to do building construction. I started to do that but three quarters through it they changed the curriculum and to have finished I would have to go full time, but I did not have the resources to do that. Then those who went purely for economic reasons hoped to accumulate enough capital to go home. And in both cases that was not possible. You were just making enough to survive.

Then you develop a life in the country and back home seemed to become a little bit more distant. And for a lot of people, early on, they got married – life could be lonely – and started having families and thinking, I can't uproot my family and go back because what am I going back to do? For myself, I got married in 1972 – my wife Janette is a Kittitian – and we had three children in England – twins Desaline and Angeline, and Marcella.

After that first visit home in 1977, I left the Post Office in 1978, and expected to go back in 1979. But, firstly, Hurricane David and secondly the overthrow of Prime Minister Patrick John kept me out of Dominica for the next five years. The political upheaval was such that my mother, who had returned to Dominica in 1972, felt and probably rightly so – she had brought me up to be a political animal – that I'd get involved. So she campaigned, and persuaded my wife that it would not be a good thing for us to come back to Dominica at the time. So it was not until 1984 that I was able to come back.

Before that there were a number of us who had been meeting in England – all of us with the idea to come back and make a contribution – Heskeith Alexander, Ferdinand Parillon, Hudson Savarin, Edison James, Lytton Paul, and myself. By 1979, all of that group had gone back except Lytton Paul and myself. Heskeith, Ferdinand and Edison went on to serve their country, the first two as ministers, and Edison as prime minister. And Hudson became the manager of Roseau Co-operative Credit Union and Dominica Health and Social Security.

Then Lytton had got together with Ron Shillingford to form an association for Dominicans, and in 1977 they invited me to come in as chairman to bring balance. That was the genesis of DUKA. Our aims were to help Dominica and also to help Dominicans in the UK – we could not receive charity status unless that was included. I served as chairman until 1982, and one of the things that happened during that time is that we founded what is essentially the Dominica National Council – we brought together the other groups, such as DONA, DDA, and groups from Preston and Reading. Dominicans saw themselves as Dominicans, I don't think they ever saw themselves, even as transplanted Dominicans, as English. We saw ourselves as being part and parcel of the Dominica experience.

The existence of DUKA was quite important. One, it gave Dominicans an institution to rally around, and, secondly, it gave us a voice in that we could go to other institutions and say we're doing x, y, z for Dominica. In particular, we were a focus in East London for Dominicans wanting to make a contribution after Hurricane David. I got myself involved full time with the hurricane effort, and worked in the Dominica High Commission office to cope with the workload. Together with a friend of mine, Joe Bastien, we used to collect the relief material and then deliver it to Wales for shipment.

But that period of waiting was one of the worst periods. I remember myself and Lytton we'd spend Sundays at each other's homes, and we would comfort each other and talk about when are we going back. After I'd left England and left him behind, when he came back on vacation he was ill and I'm sure it had to do with the fact that he was stuck in England. He refused to talk to any of us who were down here – he went through a period where he was seriously disturbed because he was under such stress and strain.

In 1984 when I finally moved back to Dominica, I was 42. The children – the twins were 10 and my other daughter was five – and my wife came down in 1985. By then I had a fair idea of what life was like and what I wanted out of life in Dominica. I did not really want a job, to be honest. I had made up my mind that I would go into agriculture. We had lands in Riviere Cyrique and so I started farming. To be honest I can not say it was a resounding success. I had problems with the terrain and secondly the work ethic was not conducive to making a success. In particular, I hadn't grown up with the land and didn't know quite what I was doing. But I knew I didn't want to live in town – it's just something I had to do. Then, in 1986 I had sold out in Riviere Cyrique and came here to Fond Melle.

I think I settled very quickly. I made a number of friends. I also got involved in calypso. Up to today I'm still very much involved in calypso. The only thing I won't leave Dominica for is the calypso season. I work for the association, I manage the stage and help run the mas camp. I also got involved for a short time in the Roseau Cultural Group and did some traditional dance. I went to some summer school classes and that was a good experience too.

One of the things that stopped me for a while being involved in politics is that in 1988 I went into the Dominica prison service as a prison officer, and having been brought up in the English tradition – when you work for government you don't get involved in a political party – you don't do that. It was a matter of principle with me. But

> ‘ If you are going to make any significant contribution to life in Dominica you have to come down and live the life. You cannot do it from out there; no matter how many dances and associations you have. ’

going into the prison service, to be honest, it has to be the most enjoyable of my working life. It gave me a chance to help persons, and one got almost total satisfaction from that experience. I did that for around nine years, until the end of 1997. Working at the prison wasn't really working because I was enjoying it so much, and I felt that I was contributing. I have continued to see the fruits of my labour so to speak. It fills me with a lot of satisfaction. I think that I have obtained a balance to my life. I've had a very long retirement, and I have been doing things that I have enjoyed.

My children settled in very well in Dominica. In England, they had had a mix of influences of Dominica and St Kitts. Growing up in England, I made sure they were aware of who they were. They didn't grow up thinking they were whites in a black skin; they grew up knowing they were black people in a black skin. And I got myself very involved with their primary school, St Paul's in Tottenham, in north London. I was chairman of the PTA. I was instrumental with my wife for introducing black books into the school – before, all the images in the textbooks were white images, and I thought that could confuse the child. That is one of the things I achieved. Then a Dominican education gave them a better sense of who they were, and the work ethic that they would not have had if they stayed in England. And my twins made history: they were the first twins to take first and second place in the Common Entrance exams and were also the first twins to gain first and second place in the CSE exams. All through their schooling, they excelled.

My experience in England gave me a broader vision of life. My perspective of life has to be different. It's less insular – Dominica is small and Dominicans think smaller. I don't say that as a criticism of Dominicans who haven't been out, but there is a tendency towards myopia of people who haven't been out. Even those who have been out to study, it's an entirely different experience to going to work – if you haven't grafted, it's a totally different experience.

Most of my set, my school friends, left and went away. The ones in America have not come back not to the extent as the ones in England. But those who stayed, I would not say we picked up where we left, but we're still friends. So I have not had any problem with any of the persons who I had left behind. People who call me English – I call them English back; it's not an issue. I try not to let what other people say or do affect me adversely. I know that I am Dominican through and through; and that is what matters from my own perspective not how people perceive me.

The people who have come down and experience a disconnect are often people who had little when they left, go up there and work very, very hard: from home to work, work to home, no fun and all they live for is working to save to come back. They then figure they must have a home and all the nice things. They send the money down to Dominica, to a relative for someone to build for them. They get glowing reports of what is going on but when they come down, the reality is that somebody has eaten their money. There is no home, there's nothing. You must experience some kind of disconnect. All your hopes and dreams go down the tubes because somebody has robbed you. So those people might want to say that they have problems because they went to England, but no, it's because they came back. There are others who could not cope with the pressures of life in England: the system did not recognise that so they pumped them full of drugs, send them to mental institutions and after a while they say, let's get rid of them, and they send them down. Here, they have nowhere to go to, nobody to go back to.

The other group are people who again have worked hard. They've come down and built their homes and local people want to think that those people owe them something – like what they've worked hard for is theirs to share and they try and abuse those people. And when you've had to put up with life in England and the racism and everything that goes with it, you're not going to lie down and let somebody walk over you. They tend to say, "No, that's not how it works." They go in to a shop, they're accustomed to good service, and they get poor service – they will not accept it. They say, I'm paying for my service; I expect to get good service. Because if I went to a shop in England and I get poor service, I'll open my mouth and I'll get good service because they don't like to be embarrassed. Here, they're not so easily embarrassed and they look at you and think, "Who do you think you are?" There's that tendency, not, "I'm slipping, I'll improve on service that I give." Over the years in Dominica, we've settled for the mediocre, excellence is not something that is cultivated and I'm talking about across the board – from the 1980s up to this day, the mediocre is king.

I hold the view, having lived here for a while, that if you are going to make any significant contribution to life in Dominica you have to come down and live the life. You cannot do it from out there; no matter how many dances and associations you have, you cannot make the impact from out there. In actual fact, the associations out there, unless they're preparing people to come down, if they're just raising funds to buy equipment for the hospital, they're just like Oxfam or any other charitable organisation that actually helps to underdevelop our country. They cultivate the dependency syndrome. I have no problem with the associations – having been part of an association and having contributed to its birth – I still want to nurture them, but they have to change their focus if they are seriously going to help their country.

What I'd like to see the government doing more of is rather than highlighting how much money comes into Dominica from the diaspora, rather they should be highlighting the need for Dominicans to leave the diaspora and come here with whatever capital they have and, more importantly, use their expertise. They will make a bigger contribution by being here. I try and encourage people to come back: even if you're just retired, there's a role for you to play.

To me the quality of life here is so much better. I say that in England only the very rich can have a home in the country and the city; I come to Dominica and I can have both. You might not find some of the things that you are accustomed to finding in the supermarkets, but it's for you to understand that Dominica is Dominica and England is England and you have to make the adjustment. That's one of the first things I did when I came down: whatever obtained in Dominica I had to go with it. Not everything in Dominica is how I'd like it to be, but in the main I love living in Dominica. I say to people they shouldn't be afraid to come back to Dominica even if they are not Dominica born. You cannot stay out there and do it, however many pounds you send down. Dominica needs human capital and that is more of a priority than the pounds. No amount of aid will develop your country for you. ■

FRANCIS EDWARDS

Francis Edwards was raised in La Plaine. He went to England in 1960 and worked for the Ford Motor company for 36 years until his retirement. He returned to La Plaine in 2006.

I was born in La Plaine in 1942 and in those days life was very very hard. We had no electricity, we had to collect the water from the river, and we had an outside toilet. It was a big, big, family – my mother had 11 children and we lived with her and my grandmother. They were farmers and we had to travel from La Plaine to Rosalie, to Grand Fond, and through Chemin Letang to Laudat and then to Roseau with the produce to sell to the huxters. I walked it many times. My father was a fisherman and I went fishing with him and we had to take the grocery by canoe to Fond St Jean and we exchanged it for salt and sugar. I didn't think about the poverty because I didn't know the difference. We always had land so we were always alright for food. Our parents were very strict and we were very limited to what we do, where we go and what we say. .

For a year I went to live with a gentleman at Laudat. He asked my mum – he was related – if I could come and live with him, but I had to do all the hard work – I was a kind of a slave, I had no freedom, and I had to call his daughter Miss Cissie and be careful what I say – so I had to get out of that and went back to La Plaine. I decided I would never never let my children live with anyone.

I first went to school in La Plaine and then in Laudat, but I wasn't learning and I used to feel ashamed so I didn't want to go to school and no one pushed me. I didn't know what education meant. When I saw I wasn't doing any good, I just called it a day when I was 14. We were so poor. Probably if I had gone further in education I would have learned a bit more about England but I only knew that England was a mother country and that my people had emigrated to England before me.

So in 1960 my uncle sent the money down to pay for my passage – £75. I took the offer because I wanted to get out. I knew cousins who had gone before me. We corresponded by letter but I didn't know what to expect. I was feeling happy to leave – to go to better opportunities.

The boat was the *Ascenia* – I think it was an Italian boat. I had a small suitcase, but nothing much – very, very little. My mother was very happy because when we went to Roseau she went with me, and she came to see me off. We saw when the big boat coming it anchored, and then I went in. We had to check in our papers and after that I went on deck but the boat was already on the ocean because it spin round. I couldn't even feel it was moving and when I look round for my mum … I never forget that because I just wanted to wave.

The month was November, and it took us 14 day and 14 night. The journey was very very rough – I had travelled with my dad on the small canoe so that helped me but loads of people were sick. I was fortunate, but at one point I think maybe we will perish. But then I didn't see the danger – the food was nice, we had wine and entertainment at night. I was so happy to get to England.

We arrived at Waterloo, and the first night I spent with my uncle in Kilburn, in north-west London; there were five of us in the room and I felt a little uncomfortable. We had no heating facility and used a paraffin oil heater. There were not a lot of Dominicans in that area – it was all spread. I loved the buildings – I was impressed – I loved the trees but I didn't like the weather because in the 1960s it was very very cold.

I sent money to my mother whenever I could afford. I went to parties, made friends with Dominicans but also Trinidadians and a few Jamaicans – but Jamaicans did not like us very much, at first they called us "smallie". It took me a long time to get used to English people – I once saw some Chinese, and I thought they were from the Carib Reserve. I didn't realise they were Chinese. We didn't socialise with English people – they didn't like black people or the Irish, it was not part of them. We used to look for accommodation – and they said, "No blacks, No Irish, no children, no dogs." They were so racist that they wouldn't rent an apartment to a black man. In the 1960s there was a lot of racism but it's died down now. Sometime I would go along looking for a job and then they would say there were no vacancies. They used to call us niggers, and we had the teddy boys – and any time they met black people they would attack them. I end up in a few fights – but luckily I never got killed.

Most of us were under the impression that it would be for a few years, but the money was so small and as you know black people didn't get proper jobs – you could only work in areas where the money was very small. My first job I worked as a porter in a hotel. The wage was something like £5 a week. In my section there were a lot of West Indians – the white people don't want that job – so it was comfortable because of that.

I stayed there for a couple of years, and then I worked as a baker for Wonderloaf for eight years, until I left and went to Ford Motors in Dagenham in 1968. I worked for them for 36 years until I retired. The starting was terrible – a lot of racism, the black men getting the worst jobs. We went there as labourers – and most never stayed because they couldn't tolerate it. If the supervisors never liked you, they just

Receiving a long-service award from Ford Motor company, England.

picked on you. These were the kind of the thing we went through. That was at the start, but coming at the end we had a proper union and the supervisors were more educated, and they put a clamp on racism a bit and said you can't discriminate. For two years I was on the production line but then I was in stock control as a driver.

I wasn't missing home but it was always the intention to come back. My first visit for four weeks was after 10 years. I love it that first visit – my mother, father was alive, some of the grandparents – I loved it. They used to admire you even when you were eating, and watch you. It was really nice. They would do everything: cook, wash your clothes – you were the golden boy. I never told them about the hardships in England – I suppose they wouldn't understand what you're talking about.

I got married to a lady from St Lucia at the age of 22 but we never made it. We had one daughter. Then I got married to a lady from La Plaine who went to London when she was nine. We also had a daughter. The older daughter who lives in Canada has been here four times, and once I took her to the small wooden house where my grandparents lived, and where my brother still lived. I showed her how we had lived, and she had said, "Dad, if you hadn't travelled you would be just like uncle." But he was happy, that's what he knew and I wasn't ashamed of showing her how I had lived before. I explained to her what I had been through and I think that has made us much closer. That daughter speaks French and Chinese and a little patois. And my youngest daughter she eats dasheen – and all those provisions, broth, smoked meat – she knows all about that and loves it.

After that first visit I came back again on vacation after 17 years. I used to have a lot of friends in La Plaine, but the sad thing is that you come on vacation and make friends but then you come back again and they had left. I would have loved to come back much earlier but when I started work for Ford, at the age of 26, I wasn't thinking of retirement. Then I got to a stage and I realised that I had to wait for my retirement – otherwise I would be losing. I took early retirement when I was 64 when I got the handshake, and used it to build a house. At one stage I wanted to live at Canefield but I found it a bit too hot – there's nowhere to hide – so I decided to come back to La Plaine. It is the same piece of land where I lived as a child with my grandparents. I built it in 2006.

I have cousins and two aunties here, but all my brothers and sisters are overseas. I've got friends all over – both returnees and others although very few friends from childhood are here. My wife is still in England – we have our house in north London – because she hasn't retired but she comes on vacation. She's got a good job and coming to La Plaine and not doing anything –she's worrying about that. La Plaine hasn't got much activity – it's OK on vacation but coming for good is different. I'm happy with my decision, but sometime it can be boring because my wife is away. But it was a decision we had to make, but there are times when it can be a bit

‘When you retire in England there's not much to do, you'd just be locked in all day …Here you can do things as you like.’

harsh. My daughters came on Father's Day – they gave me a surprise and we had a big party. But when they left I felt a bit sad.

Being in England made me a better person – I've met a lot of people over the years and we've had discussions. In Dominica you have to be with someone intelligent to have a constructive conversation. When you live overseas, I worked with all different nationalities and every day you have something to learn. Like eating – you all have different foods but the people here are basically... I can mingle with anyone from being away, but the people here are one-track minded – you hear the same conversation every day. Here you try to explain something to somebody – and if you draw attention to something wrong they start swearing at you. It's the people attitude but you have to get over that. I'm well liked in La Plaine because I live like a native but some returnees live isolated. I mix with everybody. I haven't had any problems settling back in.

I think personally that it's a nice thing going away and coming back and giving your country a face lift but some Dominicans don't like it. When they have a disagreement with you they throw it in your face, they say you got a big house and they say stupid things. I could have invested in Portugal or Spain but I chose Dominica to spend the money here. When I build this house I employ a lot of people and bought a lot of material. If you go overseas, you work all your life, you save hard; you could be a dead man, you're lucky to be back, but they don't take this into consideration. Even the government don't look at it this way. This is the only thing I think is wrong. I think they should appreciate the people who are coming and investing their money. There are so many changes in La Plaine – for the good. The only thing I am not too happy with the young generation – they are so rude. In my days, you would respect the elderly ones. You would say "Good morning" and you wouldn't swear. But it's a different world now.

There are a lot of people who came back and they couldn't make it so they went back. Some of them have health problems – there you've got the NHS. But once your health is right and you're mobile – and you can drive – you can come down. When you retire in England, you'd just be locked in all day. England's a nice country when you're working but not when you retire. Here you can do things as you like. I love Dominica, it's nice but if my family was around I would have been much happier.

One of the best things I did was to go to England because, if I hadn't travelled, I would never be put myself in a position like this. I would have had nothing. Now I can decide what I do. So it was a good decision. The other side of it was that we didn't know until we went through it what it would be like – we knew we was going to make money, but it wasn't as much because we got the worst paid job; but we got over it, and then we survived. ■

CHRISTOPHER VALERIE

Christopher Valerie was born in Cochrane. He went to England in 1961 – there were few jobs in Dominica. He was a bus driver in London for many years and was active in Dominican associations and community groups. He came back in 1996. He and his wife Doreen, also from Dominica, live in Canefield where he serves on the village council.

When I left Dominica in 1961, I intended to go to England for five years but it was 10 years before I come back on a visit and it was 1996 before I come back to stay. During my days in England, I always see and smell Dominica: some early mornings there was a certain smell, and I could almost feel and smell and see the flowers of Cochrane. In England, Dominica was always on my mind. Whenever we see a crowd of Dominicans – in a dance hall, at a party –it would be that someone from Dominica is there. I personally believe that those out of Dominica have more love of Dominica than the people who live in Dominica. The people out there are patriotic and they do a lot of things for Dominica..

I was born in 1940 in Cochrane village near to where I live now in Canefield. I went to the elementary school there until I was 15. There were nine of us in our family. My father was a farmer, my mother worked in the field. I remember my mother working for 1s 6d and my father for three shillings per day. Myself after school I went to the Ducreay estate, and we carry the oranges from the field. They used to pay us four cents for a basket of oranges which we carry on our heads.

Things were hard but we as children didn't know how hard it was, we accept everything. There was always food in the house and every

Saturday my mother would go to town to do her market and we'd be looking forward to a cake. Sundays was the only day we'd eat meat; in the week it was codfish or pig snout. On Sundays you'd have – and I still love it and cook it – rice and peas. Tea was just herbs or the peel of oranges; normally there was no milk. You'd cut some sugar cane and there'd be a press in the yard to make the juice. Everything was improvised. In those days we respect our parents, we were very obedient to elders. If you did something wrong an elder could whip you; you'd be frightened to go home and tell your dad or mam that somebody hit you for something you did because you would get another one. That's the kind of discipline there was.

When I left school I worked at the tobacco factory as a cigarette packer in Roseau for three years. I also started learning a trade, tailoring, because my brother insisted I learn something while I was at the tobacco factory. After work, we used to go to the sea, to the river... Now no one wants to stay in Roseau, but then, on a Saturday afternoon in Roseau, Pottersville, there was people beating the *bele* drums. It was beautiful. Later on you'd go to the picture house. I used to love to go there to show your strength. There would be 300 people fighting to get through a little hole for 25c. If you got in you could boast to your friends the next day, "I was in cinema last night and I made it through pit." All these little excitements were around.

I had no intention of going to England, I heard about the coldness and everything – that was the last place any of us wanted to go. My brother in law went there, spent nine months and came back because he couldn't take the cold. When I was working here I was happy: I had money, I gave some to my parents and saved some, I was independent; I had friends. But then, when there were no jobs, I said I'll have to travel to England. I had joined the credit union so I was able to get some money for a ticket. It was £72. Especially when you leave there's a bit of sadness: you don't know anybody in England. I was the only one to go from my family but my parents were quite excited about it; they gave you the freedom to make your own mind.

I travelled on a boat called the *Irpinia* in March 1961. The boat docked at Southampton on April 3 and we took a train to Waterloo. I thought England would be much more beautiful, but England was dirty; all the chimneys were black, roads were not pitched just stones like we had in Cochrane. Around Vauxhall, near the Oval, in south London, where I first lived, there was nothing beautiful about it. In those days, England was rough – you were always frightened that someone would attack you. But now I can see that we had the best time of England. I can only say that now, compared to what the young people are going through now.

My friend Allan George, who had written to me to come up to England, picked me up at the station. Two days later I was in a job. That was the exciting thing about it. I was taken to a place called Strand Palace Hotel in the Strand – I worked for £5 a week, in the kitchen. I was there for one month. It was double what I was earning in Dominica. I went to the post office and I sent £20 to my parents – I wrote and I was so excited, boasting that I'm getting double what I was earning in Dominica. But up to now the £20 has never reached my parents. My friend Allan, another young man and I we were living in one room for £3 a week; we would cook our meals – we didn't know much about English food – we put peas, Irish potatoes and salted meat everything into one pot. It's the quickest way of cooking. We used to go to the pub and have a drink – we didn't know the names of the drinks. We had a light ale; the first time we had Ruby wine. We lived together for a while until I found myself a room in a house near the Oval in south London.

After the hotel, I found myself a job next to the London Palladium at Chicken Inn. It was a restaurant and I worked in the kitchen. I worked there for four months. My mate was earning £8 a week and I thought to myself boy that's a lot of money – I have to get a job for £8. I took a walk to Euston station, it was a recruiting centre for British Rail – they told me every job was filled but finally gave me a job on the railway tracks, with trains from Clapham Junction to Waterloo. I was a member of a gang who walks down the tracks with a big spanner on your shoulder to tighten the nuts of the rails. It's the most dangerous job I've done in England. Hundreds of trains passing, the rails are electrical and you're on the track, and you have to stand in the middle of the track and then jump into the next track when a train's coming. I was so frightened. I done it for three months and then I left it, and went back to Euston station to ask for a job. I sat there until four o'clock and I just told the man I wasn't going to leave until he gave me a job. And suddenly he said, "Do you know Paddington station?" "Yes, of course, I know," I said. "If you find somewhere to live in Paddington, come back tomorrow," he said. The bus in front of my home goes to Paddington station in 15 minutes yet he's telling me if I find somewhere to live in Paddington you can come back tomorrow.

At the time there was publicity about racism at Paddington station – that they weren't recruiting black people, and the *Daily Mail* had written a report regarding racism at the station. I was told there was only one black man working there but there were two, a black skin Jamaican and a light skin Jamaican. As far as they were concerned because his skin wasn't black he wasn't a black man. We were told, we haven't got many of you guys here but if you are good workers we'll bring more of your people here. I got the job. People was coming from much, much further than me, and this man was telling me that I had to be living in Paddington – it just goes to show

On his wedding day (right) in 1964. "During the early days of teddy boys, black people were clinging together but once the teddy boys' era was over there was none of that anymore."

the degree of racism in Paddington at the time. By the time I left, it was 50% black, and nearly every black man – but not every white man – was introduced to Christopher Valerie to teach them the job. My job was sorting parcels, and then I got a job as a driver, delivering parcels all over London. The pay was £8 a week and I thought I'd made it – I'm in the money now.

I got married in 1964. My wife is also from Dominica. We moved to Kilburn and lived there in the house we purchased in 1965 until we left and came down here. By 1975, I had a family of three, and I thought I need to find a job with a good pension scheme. And that's why I ended up with London Transport – I did two years as a conductor at Willesden garage and then I trained as a bus driver in 1977. I loved it – I drove a bus all over London until I came back.

I can't say that personally I experienced overt racism during my time in England, but obviously it was there. At Willesden I was the only black West Indian in the darts team – and we'd go out together and have fun wherever we go. I never experienced any racism in my work among white people, I was treated the same. But obviously it was there. In my early years, when I worked in Paddington station, I went outside the station at two in the morning and those so-called teddy boys said, "You black so and so." We went into a no man's land, which we called mother country until we get there, and then you see notices like "no blacks" on the wall. Those kinds of things were happening but you just had to forget it and move on. The whole idea for me was to find work, take care of my family and forget about those remarks. And I always say I take the best out of everything – I'm not somebody who looks for the worst.

During the early days of teddy boys, black people were clinging together but once the teddy boys' era was over, there was none of that anymore. Black people were beginning to feel safer. In those days you could just jam into a basement when you heard music and no one would trouble you. After that, you didn't need one another, and black people weren't together again. The first few years, if you were walking down the road you'd be happy to see a black person – and you'd feel safe, but after that it was gone. They felt they don't need you anymore. We fought hard to get rid of the teddy boys, our boys fight and the law had to do something about it.

From 1977 onwards I was actively involved in work for Dominica associations in London. In the Paddington area, in west London, where I was, there was the Dominica Development Association (DDA): we raised funds to assist schools and hospitals in Dominica. It was around independence, and our first job as an association was to raise funds for the Bagatelle disaster – there was an avalanche, which destroyed many homes. I got involved from day one. I was made the social organiser and I done that for all the years I remained in England. Everything was for Dominica. I never received a cent; not even a free meal was given to us. We did it all for Dominica.

We knew there was an association called DUKA in east London and after Hurricane David we did all the packaging and sending the supplies from 510 Harrow Road, which was the main depot. It was a well-known place. From 1980 to 1986 we worked together – had all our functions, like the independence dance, together. Then there was the Dominica Progressive Association in the Peckham area, the Dominica Overseas National Association, and a new group, the Dominica Intellectuals, who were younger than us. And in 1983, we got them all involved in the independence dance. We printed 3000 tickets and sold them all. But even after telling people not to come without tickets, over 4000 people turned up. People came from Bristol, from Bradford and all over London. We had three bands and the first Miss Wob Douillette competition. It was too successful in the sales of tickets and it was the most chaotic night we ever had although we raised £13,000. People talked about it for years.

While I was a bus driver, I was also chairman of the Granville community centre in Paddington. This was a community place and actually was run by and belonged to black people. I was president of the Shrine Credit Union in Harlesden, and then became chairman of the union branch of London Transport at the bus garage. So you can imagine how active I was. Up until the time I left England, people used to call me and ask for advice – my wife said that I was like a social worker.

When I was in England I would write to family and friends all the time. I would send money especially at Christmas and my mother would say, "Don't worry about us, we are OK, you have your children." Every time I had some extra money, I came down, sometimes with my wife and the children – my three children know about Dominica and its culture; they love it but they won't come to live.

‘Many of us have come back with practical experiences – we didn't go to college to learn but we have learned certain things we can impart. We often hear people speak of the wealth of knowledge we have brought back but they never call on us to impart our knowledge.’

Like most people I only intended to stay in England for five years. It was over 10 years before I was first able to come for a visit in 1973, for four weeks. It was beautiful, a dream come true. Those days there was little pay, you couldn't make the passage money easily to come to Dominica. Some people used to take a small loan to come. My brothers asked, "When are you coming back?" I said I would come when I was 50, then I moved it up to 55. I didn't know how it would happen; at the time I didn't even have a piece of land. I had to take a loan to build and I sent the money down to Dominica, to my brother – he bought the land. I never came down to check on the building because I had confidence and trust in family. Only when it was finished in 1994 I came down to see it. In 1996 I sold my house in England, and took everything down to live in this house. Family wise we are close and we love one another, my brothers are here and that made it easy for me for my return.

Here, we need to tell people the tribulations of Dominicans who went to England – for many of us, as a result of working to maintain the home, our children are now lost to us. We had to give them to others to look after. I believe that I lost my first son because I was working every hour – it gave him the opportunity to go out and disobey his parents. We didn't have a network of families around. Then you have to get yourself involved with the police, and social workers, who had never travelled to the Caribbean and do not know your culture, coming to tell you how to raise your children. I opposed that. I had to tell them you can't tell me this, our discipline is different. It could have been easier if we were allowed to bring up our children the way we know.

The people in Dominica don't know the experiences we had in England. It was a difficult time for us – to work, to care for the children and the home, to save. And if people came to Dominica and don't have house and don't have transport, people say *ou mal twavay*, he badly work. There are people still in England who cannot buy a house. They don't realise that you have to borrow. I'd never been able to save in England because after I bought a house in 1965, all my money was to renovate it and I had to continue repairing.

But most people in Dominica think that every man who comes from England is a rich man. Mr Rich Man – that's how we are looked at. Because we have our little pension, they even envy that. They say you have your big pension and you have your big car and you don't know how we suffering here. Then they have a price for you because you are from England, and they have a price for locals. And they can spot you a mile off – even the way you walk. They say those English people they build big house and build a wall around their house – as if Dominican people never had wall around their house and some of them even build bigger houses. And some returnees don't even want the big house that they have. You give them the plan but they draft out something twice the size.

All the other Dominicans that travel and go overseas and come back they are Dominicans, but not us English. To come back and not be accepted by your own people, some people have returned to

England as a result of these things. I had difficulties with a neighbour – and he said to me, "Why don't you go back to England where you come from?" I said, "I was born here before you." He's telling me I'm not a Dominican, that I'm an English. I take no notice of Dominicans' behaviour but some people can't take it. Once they've come from England they have been called mad people – and they've had a reason to behave like that, because many people who have sent their money to Dominica to build a house, and they came down and found they had no house. Some people lost their head.

Maybe some people do cause it for themselves. You always find that. Some people who probably show off, put it on rather than be natural. That causes some friction. But it's only a small percentage of the people from England who cause them to think the way they do. There is a larger percentage of Dominicans who have resentment of returnees. You hear people say, "I hate those damn English people." They are more happy with the Americans, who come for a holiday and buy a few drinks, and they say we are mean because we have plans for our money. But most American people only come on holiday, they don't come back for good like the English. I said you should be very happy because we bought land from people who would never have sold their land – land has become very expensive because of us. They became well off because we bought their land. We come here and we create work for many by building, we employ carpenters and builders etc. You go all around Dominica and there are thousands of lovely homes. That is one part of development.

Many of us have come with practical experiences – we didn't go to college to learn but we have learned certain things we can impart. We often hear of people in authority or the media speak of the wealth of knowledge we have brought back with us but they have never called on us to impart our knowledge. They don't involve us … as much as the government ministers say they're glad that we are here. For over 10 years I have been on the Canefield council. I give my service free for the community. It's a matter of giving something because I don't want to come to Dominica and just sit there. As long as I have my health and they want me I will continue to serve. I am also the social organiser for DOWHAS – the Dominica Welfare and Hospital Aid Scheme which started in 1997. The organisation assists members financially and personally in times of need and sickness.

I could never afford to be in England all the time on my pension although I go back there every year for some months. I came here 10 years before I was pensioned – somehow I survived. Here I can eat and drink. I'm able to meet my bills. It's not a lot of money but I can live comfortably which I couldn't do in England.

Thank the Lord that I left England without being a victim of stress and illness. In England, it's very stressful. I am happy to be home, it's the best thing I've done, and I'm sure I have put five years on my life. I'm sorry for people in England who cannot make it. Here you can go to the river any time, to the beach every Sunday. I continue my hobbies – I have been playing dominoes since I was about 12 years until now. My brothers and I spend our time in the garden, planting provisions. We grow all our own vegetables. We raise chickens and pigs. That's the kind of thing we do. We go for a walk in the mornings, eat fresh fruit. What is better than that? There's time here for your body, your soul, and your mind. Everything. ■

KENNETH BRUNEY

Kenneth Bruney was born in Paix Bouche and was a teacher before leaving for England in 1964. He worked as a clerical officer for British Rail for many years. He returned to Dominica in 1997 and lives in Moore Park and serves on the village council.

Ah England. The streets being paved with gold – the books gave you the impression that England was really a wonderful place. But if you think back, what you were taught in books in comparison to when you got there – it was totally different. My first day's work was on the second of January 1965 and when I saw the conditions I decided there and then I wasn't going to stay. But then you need money. It was a labourer's job – and manual labour was not something I ever did here in Dominica. When I arrived that morning, they gave me a pair of overalls, a pair of rubber gloves and the leaf of a spring, which was sharpened in the form of a chisel. I spent all day scraping glue with this chisel and at the end of the day, when the hooter blew at 4 o'clock, I dropped this thing right where I was. I reached home without anything to eat, and then, in truth, without even bathing, I went straight to bed. When I got up the next morning, all my fingers were swollen; I could hardly bend them because I had never done anything of the sort before. When I got to work, the foreman said, "You're not working fast enough." I thought to myself, "See what I've walked into." I said to him, "I'm sorry, look at my hands." So he said, "I'll give you something else to do." And he gave me a broom and what I had to do was sweep the floor. Doing that sort of job was all the more reason I wanted to go back.

I was born right here in Paix Bouche in 1942. My father John Claude Bruney was the labour commissioner, and worked for the government in Roseau; my mother was a farmer here. I went to St Mary's Academy when I was 14 – and lived with my godfather in Roseau for four years. At the opening of school you went down to Roseau and you would not come back up until the end of term. There was no other means of transport you could use except the boat, but when they opened the transinsular road I was able to go back at weekends. My mother used to send provisions down and pay for my board and lodging; my father paid for my school fees and gave me my pocket money every Saturday. So there was no real hardship. Thinking back now life was really good, but at the time, you tend to look for greener pastures.

When I left school I became a teacher, first at Dos D'Ane and then at Paix Bouche. I loved teaching, but in the primary school you had to be a jack of all trades. The only reason I accepted teaching was that I never liked Roseau and teaching was the only thing I could do in the country. But it became sort of monotonous, and you start thinking I've got all these people over there, they seem to be doing quite well, I think I'll go to England or I think I'll go to Canada. So I wrote to the RAF and said I wanted to join. They wrote back to say that I had to be in England to join so when I arrived it was my intention to work for a few months and then join the RAF. But in those days, you needed an entry voucher to come to England; it guaranteed you work when you got there. This policy had just been introduced. I wrote to an uncle and he got me a job where he was working, at a place called Rainham Timber Engineering Company.

I left Dominica when I was 22 in December 1964 on the boat the *Irpinia*. I raised my own fare to go, it was £80. I arrived in England with one suitcase and a bit of money, and my uncle met me at

Waterloo. If I'd had enough money I wouldn't have got off, I would have come straight back. First, it was bitterly cold. You leave Dominica with tropical clothing and you could feel the cold getting all the way to your body. Secondly, I didn't like what I saw – terraced housing, things you've never seen before, smoke coming out of chimneys. And later on, I came to the conclusion that we'd never be welcome in the mother country.

I first lived in Dagenham in Essex – that is something else. It was an Indian's house. He had a tiny room, what they call in England a box room. All that is in there is a single bed. My uncle lived in the same place and we shared the cooking. At that time, I was writing back to Dominica to my mother, my father and friends: I can't really remember what I told them, but I think I said something like if I knew I wouldn't have bothered. At that time my uncle and I would send back barrels and money, especially to my mother.

After two weeks in that first job, a friend of mine took me to London Transport where they said they had a job for guards. They had a standard test for guards, which I passed, and a medical and they said, "You can start on Monday." So I went back to my job and said, "I've got a job, I'm leaving on Friday." The fellow said, "What do you mean another job? You can't do that. We're the ones who sent for you. Do you realise we can send you back?" So before he could say anything, I said, "Please send me back!"

That job as a guard at London Transport wasn't too bad. I loved reading and I used to sit at the back of the train with practically nothing to do and a book in my pocket. But when the inspector told me that I was not allowed to read at work, I told him, "This job is a dead-end job. To keep myself sane I have got to find myself something to do and that thing is reading." I left London Transport after six months when I saw an advertisement that said British Rail wanted clerical officers. I sat the exam – English and maths – it was child's stuff as far as I was concerned. I passed, had a medical, and the man said, "When do you want to start?" I spent 29 years with BR – 19 of them in Stratford, east London. I started on £9 a week. I enjoyed every moment of it. The money wasn't that much but money's not everything.

People used to call me names, but it was water off a duck's back. One time, two boys, one Indian and one white, came to buy tickets. They asked for a half fare. I said, "You're not a child. How old are you?" "OK. Give me a single, you black bastard." So I laughed, and I said, "Have a look at the mirror – put your friend next to you, and have a look at the two of you in the mirror. And although I'm darker than you, you're still black." That was normal and it didn't bother me after a while – I look at these people as being quite stupid.

My intention had been to stay for five years, and to join the RAF. But my future wife, Jessie, came up in May 1965 – our families were quite close; we met, and by October 1966 we were married. Then what happens is that you have a child and I didn't think it was worth my while to join the RAF. But I did join the Territorial Army, in the 1970s, and reached the rank of sergeant. That was great fun and if I had my life to live again I'd join the military. As far as I understand it to be a regular soldier in those days, the training was very tough and black people were victimised. Being in the TA training was two weeks per year and the odd weekend, and there wasn't time to have people prejudiced against you.

Exactly eight years after I left, I came back for the first time in 1972, for eight weeks. My uncle lived in this house in Moore Park, and the day after I arrived I stood on the veranda, looked at the scenery and I thought to myself why did I ever have to leave Dominica? And from that time on, I vowed to come back, never to leave and to live right here. That actually came true. My plan was to retire at 55, but if I'd done that I wouldn't get a pension. So from that day I decided to go for promotion because the better the job the higher the pension. In the end I was made redundant in 1995 when I was 53.

On that first visit I remember arriving that night down in Paix Bouche. It was pitch dark, and I couldn't see my finger in front of me. I found that so strange after living in England where there was electricity. I remember there were two boys on the road, and I had two suitcases. I said to the guys, "Can you give me a hand to take the suitcases up there?" One of them said – in patois – "Ah, you think that you're coming from wherever you're coming from, and you expect people to be porters for you." And the other fellow said, "If you want to help the person, help the person. If you don't want to help the person and you want money for helping him, tell him." And the fellow who said that came and gave me a hand. My mother wasn't expecting me that day so it was shock and jubilation.

I came along with a very good friend of mine who lived in Portsmouth, and we arranged to meet in Portsmouth the next day. So I got up, and put on a shirt and a pair of trousers. When I saw this friend where his mother lived, I found this man walking towards me with jacket, collar, tie, and I said, "Where you going to? You are dressed as if you're going to church." He says, "Well, my mother said, you just come from the cold and you can't go walking about without a jacket." Then I met another fellow later on and he said to me, "Where were you? You couldn't have been in England. Look at you, you have no jacket, no tie." And I told him, "When I am in Dominica, I'm a Dominican and when I'm in England I dress as an Englishman.

After that first visit, I came more regularly – although early on going on holidays and returning home is secondary if you have a family – and from the 1980s, I came every other year. By that time this house was empty. So in 1993, I got up one day in London and thought, "What am I doing here?" It was sort of a burning feeling, and I remember writing to my father and saying to him, "I want a piece of land to build a house." So he said, "Where do you want a piece of land?" I said, "Up in Moore Park." He said that I could have part of the land if I came to an understanding with my brother. Well, my brother said I could have the house.

In the latter years in England, we used to talk about Dominica more to the children. But when they came in 1976 (Kevin was nine, Jason was five) – it was just a holiday visit. My younger son hasn't returned, but Kevin has. One day I said to him, "Would you live in Dominica?" "No," he said, "although I wouldn't mind coming on a holiday". I think most of the children born in England think the same thing, and I am sure they will thank us for having a second home.

I was made redundant in 1995 and left England for good on April 3 1997. But then we lost everything we had. We had a 40ft container coming from England and it was insured port to port, not for the road part of the journey. Eventually I got all the necessary papers for the road journey but when the trailer reached Morne Espagnol the driver lost his brakes, the container and the lorry went off the road and all the contents got smashed up. We lost everything – if it wasn't bruised it was battered, if it wasn't battered, it was broken. So we had to sell our house in England to buy beds, fridge, freezer, furniture – you name it, we had to buy it. It was a long battle to get compensation – it took me 10 years and one month to get it resolved.

Apart from that, the transition was so easy because I had been coming regularly. My parents were still alive when I got back but I buried them within two months of each other in 2003. But the good thing was that I was here, especially for my mother – she lived with us. I don't think my wife was very keen in coming back, but in the end

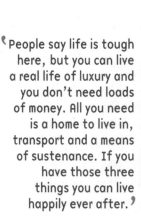

‛ People say life is tough here, but you can live a real life of luxury and you don't need loads of money. All you need is a home to live in, transport and a means of sustenance. If you have those three things you can live happily ever after. ’

she retired through ill-health and then she was able to come down. We had one son living with us in England before we moved back, and our leaving was quite a shock for him. He says that one minute everybody was around him and next minute he was on his own.

For myself I don't think I can find suitable words to describe my return. It's something that I'd recommend to anybody. People say life is tough here, but you can live a real life of luxury and you don't need loads of money. All you need is a home to live in, transport and a means of sustenance. If you have those three things you can live happily ever after. Since I came, I've planted two ackee plants. I try to grow exotic fruits. I've got three types of oranges; not long ago I planted ruby red grapefruit –and they're bearing this year. I grow vegetables. I try to help myself, and only buy the necessaries.

Out of all the time I've been here the only real negative experience

I've had is in 1997 when I went to customs to collect some doors – they said I had to spend an exorbitant amount of money for duty and storage. While I was waiting there, three white people came and then another Dominican came. I was next in line. The port manager then called the three white people in. The secretary looked at me with her mouth open, and I said to her, "It's an experience I have had before but I didn't think I'd come to Dominica and have people behaving that way to their own people." Then, when I went in to see him, I said, "Thanks for seeing me... I was there before and yet you proceeded to call them before me. I expect people in England to be prejudiced but not coming to Dominica and finding this sort of prejudice." That was the first and only experience of prejudice from my own people.

I think some Dominicans look at English returnees as people with a lot of money and the main objective is to take as much money off you as possible. I would say it stems from the fact that very few people have returned from the US – and when they come on holiday it is for a maximum of two weeks. Those from England spend a longer period of time here. Also a majority of the new houses have been built by returnees from England.

In England a group of us from this area had got together in 1985 and formed the Paix Bouche UK group. I became part of that and was secretary from 1986. We raised funds for the community, especially the church and the school. And then a group of us who had returned decided to form a branch here, so now we have a Dominica branch, which is part returnees and part local people. It would look prejudiced to have the group made up solely of returnees – it wouldn't be fair. It's for the whole community and I'm secretary of it and my wife is its chairperson.

I try to take part in everything that goes on. The first person always asked to join any group or committee is probably me. I'm also a councillor of the Paix Bouche village council from 1998. I remember one person on the council who always made a comment about returnees – they build a big house and get all their things duty free. And he always said, "I don't mean you." So one day, I really got fed up and blew my top. The other councillors never thought I got angry. The gist of what he said was true: we left and went to England and came back, but what you don't see, I told him, is the contribution we have made to Dominica. For example, my mother built a house – she would not have been able to build it without my help sending money, my brother attended secondary school and that was because I went abroad. Whatever money I sent went in to the local economy. I built a house, I used labour here; I've got a vehicle, I've got to buy everything associated with it so my contribution is more than yours. In spite of going abroad I probably was making a bigger contribution than you who never left Dominica.

If you haven't left Dominica, you don't know what the other side of the world looks like, and you get to appreciate Dominica more if you go away. I would not discourage anybody from leaving Dominica, but what I'd like to see happening is that the people who go away make a contribution to the development of Dominica. I would encourage, especially the retirees, to come back to Dominica and make a contribution. The fact that you return, that alone is a contribution. I'm sure Dominica is a better place today because of returnees.

The best thing now is that I feel that I'm at home; I know I'm at home. I remember I was coming home once and a Scottish friend said to me, "What do you mean you're going home? I thought England was your home." I said to him, "England is where I earn a living and have raised a family. Home is Dominica." I had never been made to feel at home in England. Anyone who retires and remains in England will never know what he has missed. ▪

HESKEITH CLARKE

Heaven's Best
Guest House
& Restaurant
Fine Dinning American
& Caribbean Cuisine
By Reservation Only!
Call: 767 445 6677

Heskeith Clarke was 20 when he left Thibaud for St Croix in 1964. He became a chef and went to the United States. He returned in 2004 and set up a guesthouse and restaurant, Heaven's Best, in Savanne Paille.

When I decide to go to America from St Croix I did not know one person in America, I knew nothing about America, and both me and my wife did not have a visa. My wife and I we just got married – I was 24 – and she said, "Let's go to America," and I said, "that's a good idea but where we going?" We don't know. So we went to a good friend of ours who worked in emigration in St Croix and said, "Can you give us a visa to go to America?" He look at us – he had always liked both of us – and said, "Look I'm gonna give you all a six months' visa but I know you're not coming back."

I'd been in St Croix for four years and it was like no movement – I'd gone as far as I could go. So we're at the airport in St Croix and the general manager, we was friends, came and said, "Mr Clarke, Where are you going?" I said, "We're going to America." And he said, "Where?" I said "America." Now my America thinking is America is as big as Portsmouth. He said, "Man you don't know what you're talking about man, hold on a while." He made one phone call and he said, "These people will be picking you up at the airport. Take it easy. Your works have proven Mr Clarke." When I reach New York there was a limousine waiting for me and my wife, took us to the biggest hotel, drive us all around New York and we're just looking at the tall buildings, like two people that never see these things you know.

They take us to the Lake Minnewaska Hotel in New Paltz, New York state. The guy from St Croix airport had been *maitre de* at the Queen's Quarter Hotel where I had worked, he have seen my cooking and know what I can do in the kitchen and told the people at the hotel I was the top chef from St Croix. So when I met the boss, he said you are on the payroll as from now, and I and my wife had a room in the hotel. I cried and I said, "Lord, it's not even my cooking, it is God," and I became the chef there for many, many years.

And I said, "Thank you Lord," because I remember back in Dominica, at the end of the week when I get my pay Saturday afternoon, by Sunday morning I don't even have no money in my pocket because I have to pay five dollars for my room and board. I used to come home on Saturday night after I go to the movies, before I go to bed, wash my pants and my shirt, stay in my underpants and hang my clothes out, stay in my room until that's dry, then I put it back on again. I did not have any other clothes, none, none. I used to go by the bay, I'd cry, I'd say Lord I just need your help, so when God opened a road for me, it was like, Lord I just thank you.

I was born in Thibaud in 1944. My father was a farmer, a very hard-working man, thank God. My mum she was with him supporting him. She had 13 of us. Every morning I had to be up about five o'clock, we had to take about 15 buckets of water because the river was about half a mile from our house. Then me and my other brother we had to take his breakfast for him in his garden. Sometimes we make it back to school, sometimes we don't. Come home, I had to wait for the chicken for lunch. I'm sitting down waiting to hear the chicken say "co co co" for me to get an egg for me to fry for lunch because there was nothing for us to eat.

Then, when I was about five I went to Barbados with my sister because my parents wanted something better for me. Both my aunt and an uncle which I raise up with while I was there, they raise up in Barbados. The only thing Dominican about it is that every month or so my father would send hundred of coconuts, a bag of dasheen to help her with me and my sister. He try his best because that all he had. Barbados was a struggle. Work, work, more housework. Many days I had to forsake going to school. But there was so much more in Barbados than Dominica. The standard of living was a little bit higher – that made a big difference for me, and like it was more fun, more places to go and see. I did have my toys, my Christmas gifts and everything so I did enjoy it in Barbados.

But I wanted to be back with my family so I came back to Thibaud when I was about 16. And when I came back here life was even harder. I worked with Dr Armour at Blenheim estate for a little while. He saw a difference in me – he don't want me to go and do weeding or cultivating. I worked with him and had the experience of being like a foreman. I settled back into life in Dominica but it was still difficult because the money was so small. Sometimes you could not even go twice to a movie and it was only 25 cents to get in the movie house, which we called pit, and you don't even have 50 cents.

I had a friend who went to St Croix, so when he came back I said how come you didn't tell me you've been gone. He tell me listen I'm gonna send for you. After that he sent for me and I start working straight away. I was about 20 by then. In St Croix I furthered myself in cooking, something I started even in Barbados where I was taking home economics classes. And then when I start working in a hotel, I met up with an executive chef and he saw the liking, and he start teaching me how to bake and how to make soups and sauces. The opportunity was just given to me – from a dishwasher to a cook, from a cook to a chef, and I developed there.

And all of a sudden I find myself even teaching what I was taught, it just open up to me. And I said, "Wow, I can do all of this." And then that's when, in St Croix, I got my certificate as an executive chef. When I was in America, the Culinary Institute of America in New York offered me a job as an instructor. I did not even accept it because I did not want to be tied down on teaching.

When I was in St Croix I save a dollar but I would always send a little something for my mother. Now what I did, my brother after me, I sent for him. I tell him, now I've sent for you, you help somebody else. I put him into a hotel to work, and I show him the works, teach him to cook.

America is not what people think it is. Because there's a lot of people go to America and come back home worse, my plan was to succeed. America do have money but guess what, you've got to work. I learned when I walk into a job, don't just sit down unless the boss tell you sit down. "Sir, good morning Sir. Are you hiring? I'm looking for a job." You tell him, "I'm a chef, I'm a dishwasher," and then he may say, "Well I don't have that, can you do this?" And remember when you get that job there's 50 more waiting on your job. And that's what me and my wife learned. The moment you make one mistake they can tell you goodbye.

I did not meet up with one Dominican while I was in America. I didn't have a Dominican community because I lived up-state from New York, while everybody was in Brooklyn, Queen's or Manhattan. Our social circle was mainly Americans – one of our main, main friends, he was the one who made sure I got my papers, was a New York state senator. I never personally experienced racism in America but I heard about it. One time I was on holiday in Florida and I got lost walking and ended up in the wrong neighbourhood. A Ku Klux Klan member picked me up, and I explained I was lost and that I was West Indian. He put me in his truck, told me to lay down flat because if anyone saw him they would burn his house down, and drove me to a safe neighbourhood.

We were settled in America when an old friend of mine, who was manager for one of the biggest hotels in St Croix, told me to come down. We had three restaurants by then. We opened up our own restaurant chain in the early 1980s, and every time people see me they still ask me the same question, "When are you going to open another restaurant, please?" In New York, we had two called Grand Prix and one called Tasty BBQ. Me and my wife ran them, and my two sons, who were born in New York, they were there with us too. They both like Dominica but only the youngest one I think might settle down here. The older one is more Americanised but they both love it.

So we sold the restaurants and I went to St Croix in 1988. Then after hurricane Hugo in 1989 we had to close down because the hotel, part of the Divi Divi chain, got destroyed and there was no water, no lights. We had to evacuate. I headed for the airport, and my boss got me on the second day back to New York. The next morning the phone ring, and he said, "Your ticket is at the agent, get on a plane, you're going to Bonaire." When I got to Bonaire, I did a lot of teaching, training young people in restaurant work. I stayed there for a year and a half and then back to New York again. All that time I was separated from my family – the only good thing was that anytime my wife wants to come and see me, she pays nothing nor my kids, the company fly them straight to me.

I could not come back to Dominica for many years because I had no papers to travel to come back. If I'd gone I would not be able to get back. So all that time that I was doing business up there, I send a little money home. The very first time I came back to Dominica was in 1991 – that was 27 years after leaving. Coming back was very exciting. Things was much easier. You could do things and go where

With his wife Evelyn in
New York state, 1980.

❝My wife and I we
just got married
– I was 24 – and
she said, "Let's
go to America,"
and I said,
"That's a good
idea but where
we going?"❞

you want, it was very very nice. Most of the time I used to come for a
week or two because I always had to go back to work in America. My
brothers and sisters, they were still on the island and they looked up
to me and they were well pleased how things were going for me. My
Dad was very excited. I can remember one time I got him a little TV.
So when I put the TV on my father said, "Oh my God" in patois you
know. He asked me a question, "How did the man get in there and
the man is talking." He'd never seen a TV before. And he stood in
front of that TV, when I put it on he would see that TV until sleep take
him and he just laughed.

I still had the same Dominican accent that I had over there. I never
had that Yankee accent because I never really cared for it because I

just wanted to be me. When I came on holiday I would stay in Thibaud, go down in the village and sit down and play dominoes and everything. We'd have come back much sooner than that but my wife always say that Dominica really don't have anything for us and the young kids. Leave the kids there, let them finish their schooling. Thank God we did because they both went on to do very well. Then, one day she said to me, "Do you ever think of going back home?" I said, "I'm ready anytime." She said, "OK, let's go and look to see where we can buy property."

I always wanted to come back to Dominica, always, always. I always loved my country. Dominica's giving we the Dominican people so much and I don't think sometimes we give back to Dominica what Dominica is giving to us. That was what I was feeling about coming – to give something back to Dominica. In 2003, we finally found this place in Savanne Paille. I love Thibaud as my village but business wise it's more suitable here, the location and everything.

I gave up my job in America in 2004, at that time I was supervisor for a chain of 50 houses for the mentally challenged and catering for private parties. They did not want me to leave, because even after I went back a year after, they told me your job is still waiting for you. My wife is still working in America and when we sell the business – we have a nursing home there – my wife will come down because I do want her to be here with me.

It was not an easy process to get my belongings down. Too much paperwork. Look right now I bring down one truck…and the taxes they charge you, it's too much, too much, too much. You know another thing again, you see like St Martin has duty free, this place would be loaded and crowded with more Dominicans if the duty coming back would be much easier. And here now my wife would like to bring a car down, for the family. I found out it would cost €C$51,000 in duty if she bring it down.

So I came back, set up a restaurant and guesthouse called Heaven's Best in Savanne Paille. It's tough to run a business here. In America, the kind of business I'm doing here right now, whatever I want, the furthest I may go is a mile. I could go north, south, east, west, any direction, if they don't have it here, they have it sometime right next door. You go to the biggest merchant here they don't have this, they don't have that. It is very, very hard. Not only for me, it's hard for a lot of people. But you know something I think that the people who been here all these years fit in and say don't worry about it.

Savanne Paille is not my native village but I've settled in to it very well. People treat me very well. There's certain things you have to be careful of but I still think they respect me and treat me very well. Because I'm a person always well liked and I try to treat people decent so they still see that in me. Sometimes people find that I'm too easy going. The best thing is that I came home to relax, and it's just that I didn't expect all this work. It's much busier than I thought, a lot harder work to make a living. Cause when me and my wife come down here, we come down here to say well we'll go to the beach everyday but it's not so.

I think more people should return back. Come back, get involved in something you can do best and try to teach it to somebody, help somebody to learn it. We have to learn to change and do better. I think people in Dominica really don't like changes and things have to change. Our uniform is black and white, no open sleeves, because this is fine dining and sometimes the workers come and say, "Oh, I do not have this." I hate to tell somebody go home just for that but that happen since we been here. In the States – you don't even step

‘ I think more people should return back. Come back, get involved in something you can do best and try to teach it to somebody... People in Dominica really don't like changes and things have to change. ’

in the door and the boss see you, go home and that's your last day. In Dominica they rather go to the labour union and complain, oh, he got rid of me because of this and labour gonna fight for them. Why? I mean these are one of the little things I don't like. Yes, they need to get a job but you don't want to encourage them into wrong. It's time we grow out of this, you working for a pay cheque, work for the pay cheque. We were able to employ people from the neighbourhood and the business has brought income to the area. Right now I have five or six people working for me, one time I have had eight people working for me.

I say that if you get the opportunity to go, go, but always come back with a little strength while you are still capable of doing something. Learn what you go up there to do, leave the party for later. Come back to Dominica and support the community. Dominica will change. Maybe I might not like it today because I just came from America and I'm so Americanised you know, because I spent my time there. But you can't compare Dominica and America so we got to know Dominica is gonna grow: it might not be for us, but in another ten years look out for Dominica. ■

PATRICIA BOBB

Patricia Bobb was 13 when she went to London in 1965. She brought up three children and trained as a social worker. She returned in 2007 and lives in Morne Daniel.

My mother sent for me in 1965 when I was 13. I remember leaving, literally walking from Laudat with my aunt, carrying my case on my head. It was October and I was wearing this pink nylon dress. I remember sitting on my own on the plane and then coming off the plane in London and looking at this big airport. I was very apprehensive, the reality dawns on you that I'm going to this place. Then I remember my mother meeting me at the airport, and there's this division – we were strangers, five years is a big difference in a child's life. Then I had to adjust to living with my mother – we lived in Clapton, in east London – and I never really did, and then settling into school. It's a lot of change in a young person's life. You're grieving about your grandmother and your friends.

It was never explained to me why my mother left Dominica. At the time, everyone was going overseas for a better life – an aunt and two uncles were there already. All I knew was that my mother was supposed to send for me. I remembered my auntie's husband saying, "Oh, you people are going up to England and one day they'll send you all back." That is what I heard about England – I can't remember any history lessons, we didn't have TV, and the awareness of the culture, well, you didn't have that insight. You weren't educated by your family about anything like that. My mother didn't write to me

167

and whenever she sent anything down my aunt never disclosed nothing.

I wasn't prepared for my mother leaving. All I know was I remember my mother leaving, I remember the boat in town and when she left I went to my father in Citronier. I was eight. People don't prepare you for anything, you are almost like a cork floating in the sea; you can't ask questions because no one has the answers. I didn't even know when my birthday was until I was leaving Dominica and I had to go and get my birth certificate. I never had Christmas or birthday presents – we never had that kind of life. It was as if you wasn't there.

I was born in Roseau in 1952 and lived in Cork Street with my mother and grandmother. I was my mother's only child but my father had many children. My childhood in Roseau was fun and interesting. My mother was from Laudat, and because things didn't work out when she left me with my father, I was sent to my aunt in Roseau and then my aunt and grandmother in Laudat. There, the one who I was close to was my grandmother and I went to sleep with her at night. After school, whatever she ate for that day my dinner was there, that was my granny. It was quite an unsettling thing but there was no one to complain to so you just got on with it. The negative in Laudat was as a child – as an outside child – you had to be doing so many things. You had to be doing the ironing at 11 o'clock when everyone else was sleeping; when I cut my finger I still had to wash the clothes in the river. The child had so much responsibility everyone had a part to play. The positive side of that is that it has helped me to bring up my children based on the experiences I had. I appreciate how different it is for my children growing up in England having everything at their disposal compared to growing up in the Caribbean and not having everything at your disposal.

At school in England, it was a girls' school, the class was pretty mixed – English, St Lucian, Barbadian and so on. That was one blessing so I wasn't thrown in a class where I was the only black child. I got in a lot of fights – with other Caribbean girls; you speak differently, it was name calling, and Jamaican girls went on about "small island" and so on. I eventually settled in to school but my mother wouldn't let me go on school trips. It was a very controlled thing. In England, children are living a different life and your friends are going out, and your mum won't let you go anywhere and then you find you're not fitting in. I felt very much like a country-bookie. Later on, I used to go to Dominican association parties and I think I was a member of both DONA and DUKA.

My mother had to work hard – she was a single parent. I suppose she gave me what she could, but she used to take me to buy second-hand clothes, so I wasn't getting what everybody else had, even down to shoes. Then my aunt – I had a better bond with her than with my mother – used to give me money, and I used to order things from a catalogue and I would get shoes that I liked. I started learning to sew at school and in that way I got to make the things I liked. Later on I learned from my interaction with my mother to have a better interaction with my own children, to the point of overcompensating them. From the experience of that division between my mother and myself, I made a point of never being away from my children. Maintaining family unity was a valid lesson. Dominica gave me that sense of family. I ended up with my granny but I was still in the family and somewhere else you'd end up in care and being with strangers.

When I left school – I did pretty well and did my CSEs – I had my daughter when I was 17 and then my son when I was 18. So it was like no chance of doing anything, and two years later I had my third child. I was stuck being a mum from then until my twenties, but I did little jobs in between. Then I used to work as a telephonist, did secretarial stuff, and various courses, but I've always been ambitious and did further studies. I did management training, youth and community training and have my Certificate of Qualification in Social Work.

I told my children about my life as a child in Dominica. When I was working, I told them I expect to have this done, that done, I allocated roles for them – I instilled all those things into my children: it was important to prepare them for the big world. In the UK, I did not have access to an extended Dominican family network for helping in raising children.

Dominica never left my mind, it never left me. In all honesty I never knew Dominica except for Laudat and Roseau – we never went anywhere else. But in London, you explore places with your children so when I came back to Dominica I came to fulfil and look for things that I never knew Dominica had. My mother had no interest in Dominica, she left and she never returned. She died in 1989. I used to write to my grandmother, and when she died when I was 16, I couldn't comprehend why neither my mother nor aunt came down for the funeral. My grandmother was very dear to me and they didn't make the effort. Settling in Dominica was never for them, but for me, Dominica has always held the key, it's my secret place.

My first visit was in 1988 when I was in my thirties. I came with my last son, who was 14, and my daughter who was 19. I was always going to Europe, to France, the States, and then I thought, you know what, I'd come to Dominica. I was here for three weeks and stayed with my sister and her husband. That first experience back to Dominica was quite daunting. Coming from Melville Hall – it was so amazing, it's Jurassic Park. I developed a friendship with the mountains, it was awesome. Coming in to Melville Hall is quite frightening, but I always look, even today I want a window seat because I love the view. The first time, coming down, I lived in Glasgow, Fond Cole – and for the first few days you feel you're not liking this. You're driving up this hill and you're seeing nothing but precipices. Then I went back to visit the house in Laudat where I grew up and everything looked so small. I went to my granny's place and that was still standing; my uncle was still there, and I went to see my granny's grave. Growing up I didn't get to explore much but now I go to Titou and to the Freshwater Lake – it's amazing how much water there is in that village.

It was important for me that my children came to Dominica – I brought them all down. My children know how much I love Dominica, and I suppose my daughter, who is Gabriele, the singer, would say she could never live here because it doesn't meet her needs but my grandson, Jordan, her son – he's been coming for 13 years – he loves the place. My son comes twice a year on holiday – he lives in Spain. They all love it. They have the connection. I speak patois but I encouraged my children to learn French. I was married to a Jamaican man and he couldn't do it so the only time I used to speak it was with Guadeloupean friends. I try to teach them now and because they had the grasp of the French you can teach them patois.

After that first visit, I started coming back every year, sometimes three times a year. From 1989, my intention was to do my studies and then work in the Caribbean as a VSO volunteer but things didn't work out. I got divorced in 1990 and my partner died in 1992 and so I carried on working in London. I finished my studies, and became a social worker with Lewisham social services. I worked there for 10 years, and took a sabbatical to look after my grandson and never went back.

I started renting an apartment when I came down on holiday with my three grandchildren, but when you spend so much money renting

I thought about building. I've got land in Laudat but there are all those hills and precipices, so I kept looking until I found this place in Morne Daniel. But there were problems with building. You realise that you can't rely on anybody, so I came down in 2006 and just took over supervising my building. The builder had promised that the house would be completed but when I came there was nothing but the structure. That sort of scenario could give you a breakdown or do something criminal. You feel you could really walk away because you've taken such a beating, but I had my goal. It took me a year for me to get everything done, and I did it from scratch. I had to go back and forth many many times – I thought it was the only way I could see what was going on.

The important things for me if I had to do it all over again would be to have someone to rely on if you want to build, someone who will look after your best interests for you. Don't allow anyone else to buy the land for you; and do your own research. If you entrust money to anybody, make sure they're reliable. Very often people come back and come back to nothing.

I've got a few things to wrap up in England but I'm here for good. I sold my house in London in 2007, and then started living here. I'm retired now, but I want to set up a business here – some sort of counselling service for everyone but particularly women and young people. I want to see what I can do to help, for all the knowledge I've acquired, to contribute something to my birth country. I could say that Dominica has given me nothing but I'm bringing something here, I'm responsible for people having food on their table because they've worked for me and I love the place.

Settling back this past year has been easy because I've been coming so often. When you have the mindset and you know where you want to be it all falls into place. My heart is in Dominica – it's the

'Coming back here is
about finding me,
the part of me that
loves nature –
Dominica is my home
and the place I
love to be.'

centre of my being. You can grow your own foods, drink the water,
there's no pollution; the element of friendliness. And I love it as the
nature island. It's just a matter of being; I'm free; I'm just me. Coming
back here is about finding me, the part of me that loves nature –
Dominica is my home and the place I love to be. I like the
peacefulness of it all. I experience what I had in Laudat – walking
around the village, not feeling afraid – I don't have the fears; yes, you
have crime, that's human, it's a lot to do with the influence of TV, but
I still feel it's a friendly place.

I socialise with a mixture of returnees and Dominicans who have
never left. I love the forest, the rivers, the oceans – I think that
Dominica has so much more to offer than other Caribbean islands.
What would make me happy is to see the government bring more

tourists to Dominica, improving the airlines, making it more marketable. People say Dominica has nothing, but Dominica has a lot. People don't see it; they look at the money aspect, not the beauty of the island. It's so fertile; Dominica should be the leader in farming in the Caribbean. I'd like to see young people being directed to farming. If I could get a grant from the government to do farming, I'd manage that. It's so important.

In the shops and markets you can go and talk to people, but for instance in duties and customs, when you go and apply for duty free, some of the people that should be helping you to relocate, they don't make it easy. There should be a committee for people who want to return. Getting information can be a problem. Everything you bring in you have to pay so much tax. I've encountered difficulties within the institutions but not with day-to-day persons. I've settled in easily, but the people who do create the problems are the people implementing the policies. It doesn't matter where you come from but if you speak a certain way, and especially try to be assertive, they think, we don't have to listen to that. Institutions and shop staff should have better interaction skills.

When you're away and you come back to a place, everything looks small and you understand that Dominica is only a pinhead on the map. Sometimes you wonder how the natives ever survive, especially the ones who have not travelled – their attitude towards work, their customer relations skills. You say, wait a minute, this is not acceptable. You go and buy something and because you talk a certain way they think you're English and they try and give you a different price. I have to speak patois and tell them I'm Dominican. If customer relations could be different it would put Dominica on the map but, although there are exceptions, not enough is being done to get it there. People need training – self-awareness, women's rights, women tolerate things because they think they can't do better for themselves and that's why this is the area of work I would like to do here.

You speak to some people and because they've been away they think they're better than the people here; they're not better, being away doesn't make them better people. They might have been in a better position in terms as what's been allowed them, but that doesn't make them better people. You can't be judgemental or condescending. If you have an attitude, forget it – you're going to have problems. Expect the unexpected and don't come with the expectations that you're going to have here the same as where you're coming from. Be prepared. Things are expensive – there are so many imports. People have to think of all that and get on track, maintain your focus and don't expect, because if you do, you get let down.

This is where I'm from and I think it's important that my children and grandchildren get to know what the island is like and get to enjoy it. They have the advantage of having the Caribbean as their second home. If they were all British they wouldn't have it, but they have this place where they come to see their family. Those people in the days of slavery, they didn't know where they come from. But my children, if they want to become citizens, they can.

I think the young people should return. It gives them a different view of life, shows them to see the differences between the people who have and the people who haven't. I think children growing up in the Caribbean have a better wanting to learn than children overseas because they know that education is going to be the key for the future. So if I'd a choice for my grandchildren, I'd say – let them come and go to school and let them know what's it like to be part of a small community and to exist outside the rat race. ■

JOAN
ETIENNE

Joan Etienne is from Pichelin and was sent to England in 1969 as a child to join her mother. She worked in customer services in London. She was membership secretary of DUKA, and returned in 2006 and now lives in Canefield.

I was born in London in 1960, but when I was three my mother sent me down to stay with my grandmother in Pichelin, and I was there until I was nine when I was sent to London. I remember arriving in Dominica – I remember what the hills and the roads were like and what the children were saying to me. I had a doll in my hand and the children asked me, "Where were the doll's clothes?" I said, "I threw them in the sea." Then I remember I used to go fishing with my grandmother and follow her to the garden digging up yam. We used to go and get watercress and titiwi – walking through the bushes, going to the garden. My grandmother was a banana farmer.

My grandmother had six grandchildren looking after. She was poor, but my mum used to send parcels with shoes, clothes and money to buy food. My grandmother never showed we didn't have. When she went to the garden, she would take me with her because whenever she left me, she'd say on her return: "They haven't fed you. Your belly's in your back." She always used to pamper me. I never thought about England – I was told either England was where the streets were paved with gold or it was cold and horrible, and there were no trees. That was all we knew.

It was a sudden thing when my elder sister and I were told, "Your mum wants you in England." Maybe there was pressure on my grandmother having all those children to look after. It wasn't something I was happy about. I felt, "Why do I have to go?" We went by plane and my stepfather met us at the airport. When I arrived in London I felt, "Is that my mum?" I had no memory of her. I thought, "Oh my God is that the place they want us to come back to?" London was so dark, horrible, wet. And I just stood at the window where we lived and cried. We had to stay inside which was worse because we were so used to playing outdoors with our friends. I hated it from the day one. And from that day, I promised myself I am going to get out of this country.

I went to a mixed Catholic school and was put in a class with my own age group – that wasn't the right thing to do because I was ahead of the class so I just sat and scribbled. And that put me off too. This was in Paddington, in west London, where they were mainly West Indian and English kids. So school-wise I fell behind and it wasn't to the best of my abilities. At the time my education in Dominica was better. When I went to a school in Pichelin, I was always top of the class. It was good. But in England I didn't want to be where I was, so that was part of my rebellion, I left school at 16 with CSE qualifications.

There was never any talk of going back to Dominica: my mum never went anywhere, she didn't speak of holidays – there were seven of us so there were no finances to go away. Coming back to Dominica looked like an impossible task that would never happen. Eventually, my sister saved up and she first came back on holiday in 1988 and took my son with her, he was eight. When my sister achieved it, I thought that it can be done and in the end I achieved it the following year, although I couldn't afford to take my son with me.

I had lost touch with my grandmother – after a while, because you're children, you forget about things and try to adapt to where you

Born in London, Joan returned there when she
was nine (above, back far right, with her family),
to join her mother.

are. But as soon as I started working I used to give mum money to
send to my grandmother. When I came to Dominica in 1989 for six
weeks, my grandmother had suffered a stroke – she remembered who
I was but it wasn't the same. My first feelings were that everything
looked the same. The older people that I had known all looked the
same. It looked like I hadn't left, even though Hurricane David had
passed. The majority of people in Pichelin accepted me back, but
there were times I would be called "English woman" because I spoke
with an English accent. Some people were a little hostile. In 1992,
when I returned to Dominica with my son, what I tried to do was lose
the English accent and that was better. People treated you
differently. But I felt at home and I thought this is where I want to be.

I went back to England with my aims – to come back to live in Dominica, and to see that my son was going to be all right once he's grown up. Even if it meant waiting until I was 50 or 60, I knew I was going to come back here one day. I first came back with my son in 1992 when he was 11. That was a good experience – he loved it. It was important to me that he had that connection to Dominica. I tried to teach him patois but he went to school and called the teacher "kochon" which means pig. She told him off so he decided he wasn't learning that language anymore so he gave up. But now he's older he comes here quite frequent and he has his own set of friends here and they're teaching him patois.

So in 1992, I started looking for a house to buy because I'd heard all these things about people having houses built and what would happen and how family and others could not be trusted with money to build a home for me. Then I heard about a project where you could buy your land, your house would be built, then you'd exchange the keys and then you'd pay. It sounded brilliant. So I went along with that but the whole deal fell through. I lost my deposit, but I have got the land and the title so that was one good thing. I heard people lost a lot of money – with nothing to show for it.

In 2006 I came to Dominica. I thought, maybe I can just rent for a while and then while I'm here try to build or look for a house to buy. So that's what I did. I first rented in Wallhouse, and then moved to another rental property in Canefield East. I decided not to move back to Pichelin because my grandmother had died and I felt the village was too small and the houses too close together.

I left my job in customer services at Peter Jones department store, and decided to come to Dominica, I got a job as a store manager, but I left after six months. There were times when we had to work for a whole month without a day off and times when we had to work every

With her son, David. "I first came back with my son in 1992 when he was 11. That was a good experience – he loved it. It was important to me that he had that connection to Dominica."

Sunday, with no extra pay. A lot of customers were appreciative that I had left England and had come back to work. Some people where I worked said, "You're so good at this." They really liked the way I related to the customers. A lot of the visitor customers were appreciative that I came from England too, as I could talk to them as to what to do on the streets, whether to give the beggars money or not – the rapport was quite good. I can see that I can bring my experience from England to Dominica.

I just felt this isn't what I left London to do, it was just too much. My next job was in the customer services section of a company. I had worked in customer services before so I was used to it, but there you were literally glued to the phone all day. The majority of the customers were nice but some would start yelling at you. It was pretty stressful. I did that for six months until June 2008.

One of the challenges coming back is if you have to work. What I find is that no one tends to stick to rules and sometimes holidays are not honoured. That makes staff angry because they need a break so they will take time off when they want it because it's not being given. So right now what I'm going to do is to make friends with my sewing machine. There's this thing about the environment – using plastic bags – so I'm going to started making bags out of material for shopping.

When I was in London I had joined DUKA and became its membership secretary. I hadn't known the association existed until, in 1999, I was on my way back to London and I met Kerwin Elie who told me about this association, and he said, "Come and join, we need people like you." DUKA is like a little family, you feel you belong, knowing that there are other people who want to do things for the island, you get news about the island, and meet other Dominicans.

DUKA's fund-raising makes an important contribution, but generally, I don't think Dominicans appreciate the fund-raising. When DUKA sent a 20ft container down with educational books – we spent a lot of time organising that – it sat in the docks for a long time. Eventually DUKA got a thank you note in 2007, nearly two years later. Part of the problem is that Dominicans see everything they receive as a charity, and as far as they're concerned they don't want a charity. They feel, "We've been running the country all this time while you ran off to big England and now you want to come back and give us charity and orders which we don't want." I got it from my own aunt and she told me, "It is charity alone that they're sending" about the clothes my mum had sent to her.

As far as they're concerned you're sitting in England and you must have plenty of money. Even in the work place, two people asked me for loans. I said, "I wouldn't be sitting here getting my ears bashed if

I had money." Because I drive a decent car it doesn't mean I have money – every penny I got went into it. The resentment is that the British people get five dollars to the pound, and they're jealous.

People will say to me when I tell them that I left my job, "Well, why don't you go back to England, you'll be better off." I explain to them that if I lived in England, maybe I would earn more, but by the time I've paid mortgage and so on it works out at the same thing as working here for less money. Although saying that, the prices here in the last two years have gone very high – it's actually London prices. But with Dominica wages. I brought a barrel of food down so that will enable me to survive, and then I live on provisions and try not to buy imported things like cornflakes.

I've had the odd person call me English, but I completely ignore them. Where I worked the technicians would call me Miss England behind my back. Somebody told me this so I went in there and said, "Hello, it's Miss England," and they started to laugh. Then I had one incident with a lady in the fish market. I had said I wanted to buy some fish and when I came back to get it she just totally ignored me. In the end, she said in patois "Lady, you're talking too much." I said, "What? Talking too much?" I did it in an English accent in patois. She was totally shocked and then I hit her with the song "Mwen soti desann," meaning "I've come down." And the whole market just roared. They told her, "Today you get catch that one can speak patois" and she's never done it since. Now she shows me respect. Sometimes people speak patois and don't realise that I can speak it – I learned patois in Pichelin, where it was fluently spoken although we'd get a clout around the head if we spoke it at school.

I've heard of nightmare experiences of people coming back, but I must admit in terms of the actual move and duty free I sailed through it all with no problems, except I had to pay duty on my vehicle.

> ❛For people coming back my advice
> would be that you need a proper
> skill that you can put to use
> here...I just decided I would give
> this a go and come what may at
> least I know I've done it...I'm
> really happy to be here.❜

People are encouraged to return but the government needs to have proper rules in place as to how it's done. People just interpret the rules as and when they please. Also they're too many people being ripped off in housing. There should be a real body that people who want to return can go to and find out how things are done. I know that the government asked for a diaspora policy to be done – and I was one of the people who did the survey of returnees and help put it together. It's been nearly four years now and nothing has happened. People need to know this information, it needs to be publicised.

For people thinking of coming back my advice would be that you need a proper skill that you can put to use here. When you do that you would be working for yourself. There are times when a barrier is put in place, and you also find that you have to literally grovel: you have to be nice to them for them to be nice back, and if you come across as aggressive you'll get the same back double fold. So you just have to be a nice person. If not, they'll give you a hard time.

The best experience I've had coming back is some of the people that I have met. It's a breath of fresh air, and even if they've never left the island they make you feel so welcome. They become almost part of your family straight away. Then I've got a couple of friends from here who've never left the island, and friends who were in England, like Mr Caprice, the hairdresser – I went to school with him. It just feels good being here – the freedom of being in the warmth, being near trees and the sea, being in the open air. The greenery makes me feel good.

I came with no real expectations. I just decided I would give this a go and come what may at least I know I've done it. My father didn't like the idea of me coming back to Dominica and my mum was also not happy, but my son is over the moon – he's left his whole wardrobe here, he can just get on a plane when he wants and come down. He knows that it's something I wanted to do and it's best that I just get on and do it. If it comes to the crunch and it doesn't work, I go back. The intention is to stay and I've now bought a house. My growing up in Dominica gave me a good grounds and wanting to come back here just got instilled inside of me. I don't know what it was but I just felt that I needed to be back and now I'm really happy to be here. ■

BILLY
LAWRENCE

Billy Lawrence left Dominica in 1975 for
Barbados where he developed a love of surfing
and the sea. He returned in 1992 to work as a
diving instructor. He now runs his own
business, ALDive, in Loubiere.

I left Dominica when I was seven in 1975 when my father got a job with the Caribbean Development Bank in Barbados. He was one of the island scholars and became a civil engineer. Until we left, we lived in Mahaut on property handed down from three generations on my mother's side – her grandfather had been the headmaster of the school in Massacre. I'm the middle child of three boys. My elder brother Woody and I were born in Dominica. We always used to go to the river or we were always hiking through the bush with my dad. I really enjoyed that. It created very fond memories. My dad taught us to swim very early in life. He bought us a snorkelling kit when I must have been about five. I always had a love of the water, always, because my dad loves the water.

We were all excited about going to Barbados because I think we sort of picked up on the fact that there was a tense political climate in Dominica. I thought we would always come back here because we had a house here but I didn't think I was going to come back to live. It was nice in Barbados. The school was nice although there was some teasing with regard to the accent and stuff, but I remember my dad telling me I'm gonna pick up the accent so I was always reassured by that and I did, I picked it up very very quickly. I seemed to have a bit of a knack with accents.

I remember there were four trees in our yard and my greatest thing, when I would have Bajan friends over, was my ability to climb trees and move from one tree right across to the fourth tree, and it didn't seem like they were able to climb trees. So I was kind of like this bush man. I missed the nature – my childhood in Dominica was a good one – but in Barbados, it was the sea, the beach, that became my playground.

My parents maintained that contact with Dominica, and wrote to family but the only thing they did not pass on to me and my two brothers, unfortunately, was the creole. My parents had a circle of Dominican friends through the church – that was very good in that it wasn't Bajan it was Caribbean. Of course in those days you could travel with produce like crab backs and grafted mangoes so we always had that stuff. Our family and eventually our Bajan friends would say "Oh, from Dominica, well that's the best."

I went through all my schooling in Barbados. My first secondary school was a real Bajan one. I got into technical drawing and metal work. School allowed me to mix with real real Bajans – it wasn't expats, it wasn't people of Dominican descent. And, of course, in Barbados there are racial lines, so some of the other schools would have the Bajan whites going there. It was not quite separate, it wasn't too obvious but if you spent some time there you could pick up that there were places where Bajan blacks were not made to feel welcome. And there are certain neighbourhoods that you couldn't buy a property as a black person. So I learned a lot about Bajans and how to mix – it was cool but I don't think it was the direction that my parents preferred. I was beginning to become a little bit too Bajan. I really liked that because it gave me a certain sense of belonging. I could identify with them as black people: in Barbados they would always call other Caribbean people foreigners, and people who come from England or the United States are tourists. I was like I'm not foreign, we're under the same sun. To them, Dominica is backward and I would always stand up and say "No, no, no we have nice river, fresh fruit, big mangoes, no, no impossible."

I was here for Hurricane David in 1979. The thing is we were supposed to be going to Disneyworld that year but dad had got a CDB project doing some studies on feeder roads. The way my father's house is designed allowed for air to pass through the house, which was great because it totally survived the storm. I really can't say it was a scary experience because we were working, mopping and cleaning up, but the next morning we went outside and there was not a single leaf on a single tree. We went back to Barbados soon after, and I can remember driving back to the airport thinking Dominica would never be the same again. But my dad is a very positive man and said, "It will grow back, this is how nature works, it's how we deal with it." In Barbados, I became king story teller – everybody wanted to hear stories about the hurricane, to hear about a goat pen, which I saw, completely whole up in the air and just exploding. All the kids would come around and I would tell the stories.

I was about 14 years old when I got into wave riding and that was it. Every weekend, I'd practically move into the sea. I think my parents kind of felt it may not have been a good lifestyle to adopt but they also thought that it's important for young men to be active in something. It instilled in me the never give up attitude because being a surfer is hard – the waves are merciless and you've got to have that not giving up attitude. It took me years to become a good surfer.

Every time I would come back to Barbados after a holiday in Dominica, everybody would want to see me – it was as if I had some kind of glow. I would come back with just a different kind of a vibe, a

Wedding day in 1992. "Samantha is a Caribbean woman, and is my best friend and we share a love of wanting to escape."

bit more positivity. A lot of my friends would try to feed off that. But over time my views of Dominica changed. There were garbage heaps right off the shore and everything would be dumped in the sea so I would think the water is dirty, the sea is dirty, the beach is dirty compared to Barbados. So I missed the Bajan beach. It doesn't even necessarily have to be white sand but just a clean beach. I always thought of coming back now and then but never to move back.

When I was 15 my dad asked me if I wanted to go to a private school so I went to Presentation College for two years. That was a great experience. It was very different: I was meeting a lot of white Bajans and I guess because of my background I wasn't so afraid to communicate freely with them. We shared a love of surfing, not just the water, and that became the most important thing. And again, because I wasn't Bajan, I was allowed into their circles and that was fun too. That was big cars and big houses, rich. I was very strong in the fact that I knew I was black and I always picked up on the advantages … not the disadvantages: "Hey, look I'm the only black person there, but look all the girls are around me," stuff like that.

I think I only really felt the racism when my wife Samantha – who's a white Bajan – and I got serious. We met when I was 17. It became difficult because her mother did not like me because of my skin colour, but in the end, I became her favourite son-in-law. The racism in Barbados came from both ends but it's a cultural racism. There was cultural racism in the way that everybody kind of knew their place but there were certain times of the year when there were things that they would do together, like cricket and crop-over.

When I left school at 17 – I wasn't going to be an engineer, I was going to do something with the water. I got into scuba diving and started working in a dive shop. I adapted and excelled because within a few months I was running the hotel section of the dive shop. That was in 1986. In those days, as long as you had the equipment you could take people diving. And again this knack of being able to get people to look at positivity really worked out for me. Then I started this company printing T-shirts: we'd go to the beach, surf and sell the T-shirts. I was given the opportunity to go to Toronto with the intent of going to college but I didn't like the weather. I guess I could have adapted if I didn't have a choice, but one thing my dad said was that he's not raising any bums so if I want to come back to Barbados I have to go to work.

Then when I was 22, I got into an accident and I think that's when I kind of realised that I was mortal. So that was a turning point in my life. I was driving and I had been drinking. I broke my arm but nobody else got hurt and that was amazing.

I wasn't planning to move back to Dominica, either I was going to stay in Barbados or move on to somewhere else. But in 1990, while on a visit here with Samantha, I met up with my old friend Fitzroy Armour, and he took me diving and I was just wow, OK, OK. The diving just blew me away, and I also surfed in Dominica for the first time: Dominica has great surf – it was the icing on the cake. So that changed my view of Dominica because I saw the potential of the industry and I knew I could make it here – because my roots are here. In Barbados I tried a few businesses but because my roots were not Bajan it was more difficult, my family wasn't this and my family wasn't that.

That's when the idea started forming about maybe coming to Dominica. And when my eldest daughter Ammanda was born, I did not want to raise my mixed child in Barbados. There were very few mixed children there and I didn't want her to wonder "Daddy what colour am I?" Samantha is a Caribbean woman, and is my best friend, and we share a love of wanting to escape. I think she definitely sensed that fact that I would be a stronger person here because of the roots and, having worked in the dive industry in Barbados, she also saw the potential for the industry here, too.

So we went back to Barbados and I studied to be a diving instructor. That was the plan – to study and come back to Dominica. So I qualified in 1992, and moved back later that same year, on a one-year contract with the dive shop at Castaways Hotel. It was very pleasant. Samantha is an island woman so she just fit right in. We'd go to the market and she'd have her kids and she'd make friends. It wasn't difficult. What was difficult was earning enough money, and to this day that's the challenge. The diving is better: it's like I came from a desert and now I'm in this forest – I thought Barbados was good until I came here.

At that point in time I had tiny golden locks, like a real Bajan beach boy, so everywhere I went everybody knew me. But what I didn't like is that Dominicans who knew me or who knew my family would pass me straight. That was one of the first things that hit me. The way they wouldn't come to me and speak to me or give us any help. They're there but they kind of want to see how you progress rather than put some effort into aiding. It even sometimes seems as though the system is designed to frustrate people and it does that to returning English people – "Oh that is a crazy English, let her wait, let her sweat, let her see how hot it is down here." I mean help, help don't retard the thing man. Nobody's really helping so you kind of have to help yourself. Even the folks that are here, it's really not their fault individually, personally that they're making it so difficult, it's because that's the system. You know you're sitting there in an office and everything is negative. Somebody comes in with a little bit of positivity so you try to break him down like everything else around you. Me I've struggled in other places and I'm struggling here but where else am I going to go – this is my last stand.

I am seen as an outsider because my appearance when I had locks, my lifestyle, because nobody surfed in Dominica, and sometimes because of the music I sometimes listened to. I was referred to as a coconut, brown on the outside, white on the inside, but it didn't get to me. Right now we need Dominicans to be doing this diving thing because the industry is being taken over by non locals. I think I was the second or third Dominican to qualify as a diving instructor. I left Castaways after about a year and then had a lot of fun working at Dive Dominica but finally, in 2005, I got to set up my own business, ALDive – the website is www.aldive.com – it's named after my dad's middle name.

I really wanted to help in the development of the diving in

Dominica and I became a founding member of the Dominica Watersports Association. I just wanted to see us have a united front to deal with some of the issues, because in Barbados it was a pure cut-throat industry.

The best thing about coming back to Dominica I think is family. I have a sense of belonging, absolutely, absolutely – and I'm back in Mahaut, the same area I grew up in. I live right next door to my parents – they retired and moved back – and my grandmother who I'm very close to so I really feel that I'm in the right place at the right time.

If I had stayed in Barbados it definitely would have been better financially, but Samantha and I would probably have been divorced, and our kids would probably have been living a fast life. I'm glad that I've brought my kids here. They have remained children for longer in their lives. They've had that freedom that I had as a kid. Now the teenagers want to leave to study, and they'll go to Barbados, it's easier because we all have dual citizenship.

You know this country is truly blessed, but the problem is how we are dealing with it. I think we know what we could have, but we don't know how to get there. I would rather see Caribbean people come here and buy land and start integrating than North Americans and Europeans. Unfortunately, that's not the way it may go but that's what I would rather see.

I've had one or two Dominicans saying it's good to have you back but the majority view is "You've moved back from Barbados? What's wrong with you? You have everything over there. You come back here, you bring your nice wife and your children to what, to what? And you have dual citizenship you mean you can go back and live and work in Barbados anytime you want? Why are you here?"

But then I have no regrets about coming back, and the only thing I miss about Barbados is the beaches. We are pioneers, and pioneers

'You know this country is truly blessed, but the problem is how we are dealing with it. I think we know what we could have, but we don't know how to get there.'

everywhere have the hardest trip. We don't seem to be making it easier for those who come after us. An educated child of the soil that has gone away and come back we should embrace them. Barbadians invest in themselves, and Bajan businessmen, even if they are in competition, if they have a little piece of your business that's fine, money is being circulated – they see it as business. Here I've experienced that they don't want to feed me because they're afraid of getting their hand bitten.

We have basically put everything except our lives into our business and it's very scary – financially it's a really tough challenge. If other young people come back, they must know that nothing will come and drop on your lap, you've got to get up and move yourself. You have to come here with the confidence that you're going to be here to stay. I really try to encourage people when they come back. I'm like we need you because how is it going to change if you don't come back? ■

STANLEY PAUL

Stanley Paul had lived in other Caribbean islands, playing cricket, before he left for Canada in 1993 with his Canadian wife. He became a worker for people with behavioural difficulties. He came back in 2005 and lives in the Layou Valley.

O h boy let me tell you when I reach in Canada – that was something else. I went in the town and all I saw is white, and so my first few nights for a long time, it's nightmare man … that was tough to get adjusted to. That was a culture shock. For months every time I close my eyes is just millions of white alone I seeing. And when I say white, I mean even those who are East Indian, they all white to me because so much of it I couldn't differentiate. If the thing wasn't totally black, like Negro black, it was all white to me, it was like one colour. That was Victoria. It was all the way past Toronto where all the black West Indians go, Toronto and Ontario and those places, I mean even Vancouver some people there, but not right down Victoria right on the west coast.

Everything was different – I couldn't understand why everybody had a chimney in their house, I thought it was like a bakery they had, and it's not a bakery man it's somewhere to get warm, to burn wood and ting. And I was wow! Everything was different, the food, well it took me a long time to eat. I asked for fish, first time I went to a restaurant, it wasn't long after I reach. And I watch the menu, well, I had no idea what I saw, all I see is different names I had never seen in my life. Holy Moly! It doesn't make sense to ask a question because first thing they're going to know, well boy you're not from nowhere close, you come from somewhere far, and if I tell Dominica, then they have no idea.

So I ask my wife Gail, fish, fish, check me a fish and ting. So when they bring the fish, they bring salmon but salmon now is like pink, and I'm checking, I say no way, no way!!! I said I want fish and all you bring that pink, what all you put. They tell me no, no, no that is the colour of the fish and everything. And I said what!! Pink fish, no way, I don't want that. So anyway they coax me, they say try, I had a hard time eating... And that fish now, boy once that pass by me I want it. Imagine, I went and fish those things. I tried everything, and in the end I like Canada, I'm Canadian you know.

I was born in 1960 and grew up in Layou, in my father's village; my mother is from Morne Prosper. It was cool growing up, nice man, I enjoy it. It was the place that had so much fish and the capital of titiwi. I mean Layou have plenty things that different than other villages in Dominica. I went in that river man, I in that sea, I explore it. Going in the bushes and hunt down the little animals, birds everything, you know what I mean. Eating fruits.

My mother and my father, boy, they did a lot of different work *oui*. It was hard for my parents, up to now. It look like you never have enough money, but there was always food, because we always have plenty land. It's not the same now. For example, the people now that are about 80 years, they need somebody to sleep with them. But their kids – like the mams that are my age and the dads – either they're not responsible or they can't control the kids because when I was a little boy I had to go and sleep with my grandmother and I never had to complain. Your father cannot go there, he's a big man, he have his house but he have children so they can represent him by their grandmother right. Well it's so it is.

There was more togetherness in working in those days. For

example, this is the heart of one of Dominica most well-known area for bananas. When you watch now most of the farmers that used to occupy the land there they died, or they're sick. But then the kids of those guys they are not there, so there's a lot of abandoned estates and holdings. Some of the kids they go to England, America, wherever and some of them even here, it's just not the same.

I never really say in my little boy days having problem with the community you know. But now I think it's different. Let's say our children, the people at my age, their children is the one that causing most of the problem in Dominica. Somehow I don't know where they went wrong. And I think the finance for them is much harder now than it was for our parents. And the inauguration of television and those things, people always want more. So that creating a problem. And then Dominica have to compete with the world. Even though Dominica doesn't have natural resources it must raise up it tax and you know there is not much people to raise up tax, so the people there struggling.

Well I did my schooling in St Joseph and then I went to a polytechnic college down in Mero. They used to teach us skills you know, electronics, and whatever, practical skills. And then I went to take lessons at the Academy and then at the University of West Indies extension. There now I was learning political science – just young man trying to get knowledge. I studied religion in Trinidad and did a bachelor's degree course in theology. I was born Catholic but my parents went to Adventist one time and then Christian Union Mission, and I wanted to understand what all those things about. To me knowledge is always power.

I was happy to be in Trinidad learning, and playing cricket. I was doing so well in Trinidad you know, my mindset was on West Indies cricket team. There was a little book the fellas wrote about me – as

At a cricket culture festival in Vancouver, Canada, 1999.

the next Michael Holding and so on. I used to play very well. So I've been around. And then in 1979 I just left my studies because, in Dominica, Patrick John was going to overthrow Miss Charles and I run back. I saw Dominica looking very unorganised. When I came here I got a job right away, working at the public works office in Layou as a timekeeper. I decided I not going back Trinidad anymore, to do no schoolwork or cricket. I just stayed in Dominica for one year.

After that I started playing cricket again: I go to St Thomas, St Croix those places and I played cricket all the time until about 1992 when I met Gail, who is from Canada. I don't know how to call me, professional or what, but they used to give me money – if I wanted an old car they give it to me. In 1993 Gail and I decided to go to Canada and when I reach Victoria I started representing British Columbia province in the North American championships. And I represented

Victoria against MCC England twice. So I play a lot of big games there against a lot of Test players. I enjoy that.

Even before meeting Gail, I had it in my mind to leave Dominica. The idea was to work, come back and build, which is exactly what I did. Go work, don't gamble, don't spend it in drugs and women, save it, come back and get a little peace of mind in Dominica. And build with the intention to help one or two people down the way, like open a little store, something you know to get two people employed. Well as you see I have somebody employed in the garden, so I like that. I first thought I can go five years, make enough money and come back but not for many years I was able to come back.

I didn't really have a proper idea of Canada. But it was totally different than what I had heard. I didn't hear much what it was like to be a black person in Canada, not much to get scared. I think I was naturally more scared of the United States than Canada because you hear on the news all the time what United States look like. I would never be scared of England though, I would love to go to England, cause I have family there. I even support England on the cricket team right now, though I'm West Indian naturally.

My first job in Canada was painting. I like those things during the summertime but as soon as the winter started I noticed my body was always feeling different. Swell up fingers and everything like that. After the painting I did construction, then landscaping. I loved the construction the best you know because you're more creating. After that I decide, well, I need to do something different because I need to make money and so I went volunteering in a day programme, where they're teaching developmentally challenged people different skills. I wanted to go to the Camosun College in Victoria and part of the prerequisite was to go and volunteer to see if you really make up for that job and if you like it. So when I went to volunteer and they gave me a job. I didn't even have to go to the college so I did all my training on the job. So I become like a specialist in behavioural support for the developmentally challenged people with neurological problems, like Prader-willi, Down's syndrome, Rex syndrome. I worked with the ministry for family and children, with doctors, lawyers, police, all kind of people. I was a programme facilitator for developmentally challenged adults. That's what I doing up to this day.

For me the adjustment was going in a foreign land and learning to cope with all the different ups and downs. They do things differently and then you have to make up your mind you have to go through a struggle too, you know, to make it. Now it's the same thing with people that lived in Dominica in their early lives and they go to England and then they retire and they want to come back home and they didn't come back often. They never really come back to Dominica often enough to get accustomed to the changes. Suddenly they just come back and then they want to bring back a mini England with them in a poor country like Dominica that don't even have a skyscraper. There is a difference, so that killing them. So when they come they think everybody either lazy, mad, scary, not like the British guys. So they run back or they die quick, they cannot adjust right. You always have to remember Dominica or St Lucia or wherever you come from in the Caribbean, to love it and appreciate it and don't compare it.

Every two years I try to come back to Dominica. Every time I come back, my friends and them and all the children can always recognise me and it's like I never leave. Once I come in, I in Dominica, I is here, I home. Because I tell you I'm in tune with the people. You have to come back and know them. Anytime you go and you don't come back, people are building their opinion about you. They saying, "Well

> ❛If you living in Canada, or England, anywhere, have your country in mind man and don't criticise it and don't trade it for something else because you think that thing else is better than yours – it's not really better, everything is different.❜

you see mister up there, he don't call, he don't write but when you see he come down I don't want to deal with mister eh, because mister is this and that."

Some people, when you're from England or somewhere, you're studious, you want to know well you cannot use past tense for present tense, you cannot just use any word. Those guys not used to that: Dominica is any word goes as long as it makes sense. But the guys don't want it so. And some of them do adjust, with lots of family members and good friends determined to help them through their grumpiness and whatever.

During my time in Canada I try and support my family. I also adopted my second sister first kid, I adopted him at 12, he's in Canada, he's about 25. I send him to school in Canada, everything, make sure he graduating, getting job, he's doing good. I contribute a lot you know to the system. I took my father for a visit in Canada. My mother will come one of these days.

I always kept in contact with what was going on in Dominica all the time, through my family by phone. My first few years I went to Canada, I probably wrote about 160 letters I only get one – he died now, an old man had write me back, we called him Uncle Sam. And when I come down to Dominica everybody say, "Boy, I got your letter man ... I wanted to write you man but...I still have the letter you know." So I said to Gail it doesn't make sense to write letter. So if I get a chance to call one man I tell him to say hi to everybody.

If I have to sit down and talk about the goodness I got in Canada versus the racism, the goodness I have to take about the rest of my natural life to talk about it. The badness is not something I really worry about because there is always in every country some idiot right. There were people from all over the world except Dominica, people from lots of the African continent that playing cricket like Kenya, South Africa because we have a cricket community there, so there's always cricket.

I always try to be Dominican no matter where I go. I teaching people with problems to have good behaviours, so I like to maintain who I am so you can just accept me for who I am. But there is a difference that some people notice: when I go down to Layou some people will say that certain things I say that is just like a Canadian.

I started getting fed up with work in Canada after a while. After years in the routine it become like wow, you need a change. There was a time I was working seven days a week on two jobs. Especially during the winter, stay inside watch TV, read a little bit, back to work in the morning. So I came here, got the land in 2005. I tell Gail let's go down, I just leave my work and I go down. Gail was happy to come back to Dominica, it look so to me – she hasn't told me for us to go back. It was important to come back to this area because that's my area, I love my area, I wouldn't live in Layou proper but I have to be in my constituency.

But the thing about my work, it's your reputation eh, I could just go back now and I getting my work. They thought I had a gift with dealing with developmentally challenged people in Canada. They thought it was my language and they thought it was my locks or my

"It has its ups and downs but I'm happy for being back. It was nice to get away from all that bustling in Canada, it's very stressful up there."

colour. So they had interviews with me to figure out why and I just tell them well you know what I mean, maybe God just want me to do it, or maybe...I respect people. People in Dominica sometimes don't have an understanding of how to deal with problems like Down's syndrome. That's where I come in; I develop programmes to teach the awareness of it. Well right now, Canada is so well organised because they're getting the problem right in the hospital. In Dominica, lots of those people never found their problem in the hospital – you go home, your baby healthy but it's a Down's syndrome with lots of behaviours and difficulties. And then you alone on your own. In Canada it's not so, you get help and assistance.

But in Dominica you cannot pass on those skills because the

infrastructure is so different. I think Dominica has a problem because they don't utilise the skills of people that go to the first world, let's put it so, and develop nice skills that can be used here; they don't understand those things. If I see a man in a trouble I try to help him. If I go down the road and them little high school children meet me, they tell me Paul that is something hard but I could understand you boy. I take out my book. I show them how to do things, drawing, writing, everything. That is the way I can do it.

As I said it has its ups and downs but I'm happy for being back. It's nice and fresh; it's quiet where I live. It was nice to get away from all that bustling in Canada, it's very stressful up there. And I want to establish myself here too, you know. We have some crops here already like the mangoes, the cannelle, the nutmeg and the breadfruit, grapefruits, oranges. I re-establishing the bananas and the plantain and just trying to make there a nice little pleasant place to cool out. I thought about the work I did in Canada but it probably would take me another year or so, when I settle down a little bit more, because it's demanding. But I wouldn't want to go and work in the physical aspect of it, with the individual, I would rather work with the workers or the staff, training. I can help them with the computer to develop training programmes.

The down thing about being back is that you have to have patience. And you have to figure out the shortcuts. For example I'm trying to repair a house down in Layou so that I can build a shop and everything there. Then I have to wait a long time for certain things, it's not easy… but when it happens, boom, you know. So that is the down I find, but that is the way it is. So I learning too, OK, it's Caribbean time, take it easy, it will happen.

I think the government should encourage the young generation to leave Dominica and encourage the old ones to come home. That sound backwards but it all have to do with politics. Because it doesn't make sense to encourage all the young ones to come home and when they reach home there is nothing to do. They're young, they need money. Go out there and spend 17 years, because most of the young fellas that didn't go, I come back now and I meet them the same way, didn't have that opportunity to go. Pretty smart fellas, pretty nice guys...

The way I watch it I would like to encourage everybody that is a, let's use that word, foreigner, in a strange land, like if you from Dominica and you living in Canada, or England, anywhere, have your country in mind man and don't criticise it and don't trade it for something else because you think that thing else is better than yours – it's not really better, everything is different. So come back home man and help me to build, me and Gail we're trying our best, so come down with your money and build the country. ∎

PHILBERT AARON

Philbert Aaron was raised in Portsmouth and left Dominica to study in Africa and the United States where he lived for 12 years. He returned in 2008 and is the ambassador to ALBA (the Bolivarian Alternative for the Americas) set up by President Chavez of Venezuela.

I was a happy kid – I had a lot of freedom, like many children back then. I was able to swim in the sea, go diving, snorkelling, sailing, fishing, go into the bushes setting traps for birds, in those days you could do that. We also went to the garden – those were the things that occupied your time.

I was born in 1962, we lived in Lagon, Portsmouth, and my parents were farmers; they were squatters on government land at Brandy, east of Picard, two miles away from where we lived. We would go out with them, and plant a tiny garden. We would weed and dig, and carry on our head produce such as bananas, plantain, dasheen. My mother was also a seamstress; she had an old black Singer sewing machine and would sew clothes for the family and would take in sewing from others for a fee.

Life at home was organised around chores. We did not have piped water so in the morning you would go to the public standpipe on the road side, wait your turn, fill up a butter tin or a plastic pail, put it on your head and go back home. I also remember sweeping the yard; sometimes you would feed the livestock. We also went to gather fruits, for fun or for subsidising the family needs. All that was done before you went to school.

Being basically close to peasant farmer status, you are

apprenticed into the activities of your parents based on gender – so my sister learned to sew and to cook and wash – I did not. I learned to farm and also to fish. We were definitely poor and to say working-class is even too much. We didn't even own our own land so we were basically squatters and fishermen.

I was keenly aware of our class status, perhaps more so than the rest of my siblings, and I still am. I was aware of it from very early, and I saw it in school. There was an incident that I've never forgotten where I was punished by the school for something and I felt it was because of my station; I didn't have the vocabulary or conceptual understanding at the time but instinctively I understood that. And, of course, there was also a landed aristocracy in Portsmouth – it's ringed by estates – so I was always aware of that.

It is interesting that at the time being in a lower class had virtue and it was the reason that you worked harder. When I started studying education, I was shocked to find that sociology science had established that students from working-class and poor communities in principle perform less well than middle-class students. It was a shock because that was not what we were led to believe. Although we knew there were differences, we spoke differently and so forth, that didn't limit us in what we thought we could do. And that would mark my life very much because my class background – and chasing yachts – has had a lifelong effect on me. So that kind of class awareness, which also tied in with the politics of the time, did make a big difference:

I was what was then called a "chase-I" – now called, respectably, a tour guide. Someone who would row out to the pleasure yachts in the harbour in Portsmouth and offer services, whether they needed fruits or wanted to go up the Indian river or you'd arrange for an around the island tour. So I did that with friends or on my own – my father being a fisherman we had a familiarity with boats and built our own.

Chasing yachts was very exciting – you met people from all over the world, you conversed with them, there were no limitations in what you spoke about; they exchanged books, magazines, beautiful clothes. As a teenager in the 1970s, I remember wearing Lacoste and Fruit of the Loom clothes when no one in else in Dominica did as far as I know. So being a chase-I gave me social skills to deal with many people. It taught me how to work, how to do business, how to market myself as well as marketing goods and services. And it taught me politics.

I went to Portsmouth secondary school and for a long time school life was very boring to me. I didn't perform well at school at first. The things that were fun were the chores that I did, and especially the freedom I had. But at school I became friendly with a wide spectrum of people and my social life was very interesting. My friends ranged from those who are now well known political figures to some who are in jail or strung out on drugs. Later on, in our teenage years, a few of us would become members of the Dominica Liberation Movement Alliance.

I am one of the very few people in Dominica who worked their way through high school. I remember paying €C$85 to take my GCE O level exams and before that I had been paying for books and other things. After leaving Portsmouth Secondary School, I worked for a little while as a teacher there to earn some money, and in 1980 I went to Sixth Form College in Roseau using the money I had saved.

Just about when I am finishing school I get interested in politics and I speak on a platform for the Alliance. At that time the Black Power movement was dying and some of the same figures had moved into the rising Alliance. One of the things that was attractive to me about politics was the idea of a class struggle. I was not very interested in the racial struggle. Only the Alliance had the class struggle as its main programme. I was also interested in the "life of the mind" – with the ideas the Alliance leaders had. It did not campaign like the other parties; it was involved in a different kind of politics, which was the education of the electorate. I became interested in how different groups become conscious, what makes for political success. Understanding that is a key thing throughout my life.

At the Sixth Form College, I worked very hard and succeeded brilliantly. So I'm starting my educational success at a late age. There were very few possibilities so I become a teacher of French and Geography at what was then the St Joseph campus of the Dominica Grammar School. Because of that I would be sent in 1983 on a three-month attachment in Togo for teachers of French as a foreign language. At the time, my knowledge of Africa was bookish – you did not speak much about Africa in Dominica. But again because the Alliance members had been interested in Africa, we passed around books, so we knew about Africa's mineral wealth, about the good guys and the bad. But I did not know too much about Togo except through a song by Exile One.

Before going to Africa a key thing happened and set me up for Africa. In 1980 Mary Eugenia Charles and the Dominica Freedom party win the elections with US support, trouncing the Labour party and the Alliance. And that becomes a huge philosophical disappointment and a philosophical question for me. How did Eugenia Charles, a woman who was wealthy, from the planter class, manage to get working and poor people to vote her in, in a landslide, throwing out the Dominica Labour party which had been a pro-workers' party, and worst of all why did the Alliance not even come close to winning one seat? That would be the question that would push me to Africa and it still marks me today and shapes my academic work. I had been reading Leopold Senghor, president of Senegal and a poet, and Julius Nyerere of Tanzania who had begun to think about the failure of Marxism to even catch on in Africa – and they were basically saying there is a culture that is a barrier to Marxism-Leninism.

I grabbed the opportunity to go to Africa to learn about roots, to learn about culture – I learned that Dominicans had come from Togo. Also during my years chasing yachts, my American friends would say how entrepreneurial we were being, would praise the "can do" atmosphere among us and they would always advise against coming to the US. They did not hide issues of race. Many were out here on their yachts precisely because they disliked the values of America. It was a yachtsman who gave me a copy of Alex Haley's Roots, for example. And another advised me it was just such a terrible place for blacks. So at the time I was very receptive to Africa.

Those three months changed my life. By the time I came back I had to admit one thing: I had very few opportunities to further my studies in Dominica. So I would return a month later to Togo and start a bachelor's degree in French – at the University du Benin in Lomé. I spent four years there. They were great years. It was a whole new world.

One of the questions that I took to Africa was about religion. One of the main things in the explanation of why the Freedom party won in 1980 had to do with religion – the Catholic church was involved in a very direct way in the campaign. At the time there was a major ideological question that Marxist-Leninism was atheist, and it was felt that black people, especially Dominicans, were inherently religious. I would learn in Africa that black people are not inherently religious, they might be even more secular than white people, very matter of fact, very rational (except for West Indians and people in the New World, who maybe because of their experience as slaves, are more religious). That understanding was a huge liberation for me and explained the success of the campaign of Mary Eugenia Charles.

I came back in 1987 from Togo and again started teaching French at the grammar school. I had always wanted to be a teacher of some sort, a university professor, but of course Dominica didn't have universities. Working-class people do not usually jump from being farmers like my father to having very liberal professions, like medicine; they usually go through lower level, middle-class professions like teaching and that was probably the horizon I had in mind. I also like teaching because it also gave me time to write and think.

I thought of moving away because I had been exposed to so many different people as a chase-I. But I never thought of migrating to live and work – I thought I'd go away to study, which is a different kind of thinking. Although I didn't think of living in the United States, it was always more attractive to me than England. A lot of my uncles and aunts went to England in the 1950s; there was no one I knew who went to the United States. The Americans I met as a chase-I were, as a culture, more elegant, that is the word you would use. Maybe there was more money, the way they did business, the design on the US boats, the engineering and the clothing. England never attracted me at all.

The uncles who returned from England didn't give you a peek into what was going on there except for one uncle, Uncle Eldon, who had a major influence on me. He worked in the post office in England and returned to live in Dominica in 1980. He's an amazing man. He had spent a lot of his time studying, especially western philosophy, so when I go to the Sixth Form College he helps me to succeed. And he begins to unmask what England is. I would go and visit with him every Sunday and we would gather at my granny's, and he would walk me through the labyrinths of western philosophy and music. He introduced me to Billie Holiday by way of London! My uncle lives a very simple and beautiful life – he does not drive cars or build a huge mansion. And he explains some of the class issues that there are in England, and draws my attention to the special condition of returnees to Dominica who wither away within a few years of returning. He lifted the veil on what immigrant life in England was like and that influenced my decision not to go.

In 1990 I earned a Fulbright fellowship to do a master's degree at the University of Kansas. After two years I came back to Dominica and spent nearly two years, again teaching. I was teaching reading in school but I also set up my own practice as a reading specialist, teaching kids of all ages to read. Then, in 1994, I leave again and go back to the US. This time my quest is to get a PhD. I did my PhD at the University of Maryland, and the issue that I study is social class as it relates to education. And my own life, I think, is a good experience.

In the United States, I retained my ideas, my individuality. I do not blend in or lose myself but I fit in – again it's thanks to the social skills I learned chasing yachts, and that social skill is a key thing that helped me navigate the US in a way that is seamless. I had a very successful experience there. I did not experience any overt racism. I had no experience of that. So that's pretty beautiful. While I did my PhD, I was a research teaching assistant and later became an assistant professor.

By no means did I abandon my Dominica roots – I keep reflecting on Dominica, keep contact with home, and with the literature and

> ❝ If all of us who return
> emphasise the will to adapt,
> to be receptive and tolerant,
> it may act as a catalyst for
> others. It's a mindset we
> have to exhort. ❞

culture of Dominica. I also maintained Dominican friendships in the United States and became a member of the Dominica Academy of Arts and Sciences (DAAS).

It is difficult to say exactly how my personal experience in the US might have been different from those of my relatives who had gone to England. There may be several reasons why it may have been easier to integrate in the US. For instance, my relatives migrated to England at a younger age than I went to the US. That is important. One of my uncles describes going from a very rustic boyhood in Guillette into the heart of London, Victoria station. After visiting Victoria station myself, I could imagine what an alienating experience it must have been for a simple boy from Guillette.

Also we migrated for different reasons. Some uncles went to England to find work or make a better life in a very direct, economic way and I migrated to the US largely for higher education. And there is no better way of transitioning into a foreign society than through school. I may also have been better prepared for the culture shock than my relatives. I had been a chase-I, a tour guide at Portsmouth. That began to socialise me into some of the mannerisms of Americans. The Americans I worked with did not hide the issues of race that existed in the US. And that is partly why, before I went to the US, I had lived in Africa and that also helped me to transition better. Lastly, I benefited from the earlier generation's experiences in

England, especially my Uncle Eldon's. He let the cat out of the bag on what living in England could do to the mind of a black West Indian. And he would point me to psychiatrist John Royer's study Black Britain's Dilemma, and I began to glimpse at the torment of being black in white England. That helped me to ready myself for the assault of immigrant life.

When Uncle Eldon returned to Dominica, he went on to live an active political and civic life in local government here. That was inspiring to me. So although I always intended to come back to Dominica, it firmed up my commitment to coming back to Dominica and making a contribution.

Dominica as a sending country was also different for each generation. You have to imagine what Dominica in the 1950s must have been like. A Dominican immigrant to the US today is already socialised into American life by way of television. He has easy telephone contact, there's the internet and so on. Then, he might return ever so often. That makes a huge difference.

I had a time frame to come back – I wanted to come back in 10 years, in fact, I came back after 12 years. The main thing is that the woman I love lives in Dominica and had no interest in coming to the United States or living elsewhere. The second thing is that I'm a writer and I do my best work in Dominica – it's the ideal place for writing. So it was a very easy decision to come back. I didn't think about how I would earn a living, I just felt everything would fall into place. I had no concerns about coming back because I had trained myself, as a writer, that the challenges of life in Dominica are what I write about and think about.

My Dominican friends in the US were thrilled that I was coming back – many would like to come back but feel that they can't because of where they are in their lives and their expectations. But they were very supportive. Many of them confessed that they had been putting off returning for many years, they had been saying it but not doing it. I had been very planned all my life, and had been very methodical of what I wanted to do. When it came to coming back I just let go. I think it's a state of mind. My American friends were very excited – they liked the idea; it's a very romantic idea for them. And my family were very excited – my mother was so very very happy that I was back. Not one person thought it was the wrong decision.

I came back in January 2008 with no plan for work, but two months later I became the ambassador to the ALBA, the Bolivarian Alternative for Latin America and the Caribbean, and co-ordinator of ALBA projects in the prime minister's office. It's a very exciting job, and I enjoy it a lot. The practical move of coming back was the easiest thing. No hassles at all.

I studied policy and right now I'm in a policy position. This position ties in social skills that I learned chasing yachts, and the political skills I learned, especially understanding politicians. That combination – an understanding of policy and how it works – is what I bring to this job.

I've had no problems coming back. There are little hurdles that everyone faces – for example some things should be faster, setting up a bank account as a returnee can be a challenge. There are those hurdles but it has been a beautiful re-entry. People have been very receptive and very supportive – and I think it's because I maintained a certain kind of connection with Dominica. I've always remained focussed on the issues that Dominica faces. People recognise that I'm not new to the game so on an intellectual level I never left Dominica and Dominica never left me.

Rather than focussing on those who leave, I think we should focus on those who stay and those who are coming back. And they're making interesting contributions in very interesting ways. If we focussed on that it changes the entire picture.

I think the diaspora already plays an important role. It's having a major influence not only in remittances but in the interchange of ideas. Contact is already going on between individuals overseas and here, there are all kinds of channels.

It seems to me that there was greater structure in the migrations to the UK. It had much more of a generational shape to it. More Dominicans in a similar age group left at more or less the same time. This would mean that they might retire and then return in larger numbers. On the other hand, migration to the US is more haphazard, more based on family or individual access, and since migration to the US happened later, then it seems logical that returnees from England would have a more dramatic effect on Dominica.

I've heard cases where people have had conflict in returning but if we emphasise the will to be flexible that takes care of any possible problems. People who are receiving you recognise your willingness to fit in, while also respecting your individuality. If all of us who return emphasise the will to adapt, to be receptive and tolerant, it may act as a catalyst for others. It's a mindset we have to exhort. I don't think it's the kind of thing that lends itself to programmes. A special programme to reintroduce this group into that would not be elegant and would need a structure – and it creates labels.

I would just advise people to come on down, keep an open mind, be flexible, and come. ■

ROBERT
JOHN

Robert John was born in England and first came to Dominica when he was seven (above, left, with mother and brother). He was a corporate software engineer in London before settling in Salisbury in 2006. He is setting up a company to manage builds for returnees.

I was born in London in 1968 and my first visit to Dominica was in 1975 when I was seven and we spent the whole summer holidays with my great grandparents in Salisbury. Coming here was almost like a sense of belonging – it was clearing up a mystery. In England, there were lots of things you didn't understand, even if you followed and believed in them, and then coming here you could understand how your parents did things in a certain way. In terms of the strictness and discipline, you saw it around you in Dominica; how the other kids behaved towards elders and adults; the freedom; how kids roamed and their pastimes – catapults, swimming in the river, climbing trees for fruit. In London our parents kept a tight rein on us; we didn't go out of the house much, we were too young to go out. But here cousins took us everywhere. Once during that trip, we were in St Jo, my aunt and mum went to Roseau and I walked from there on my own through Layou and over the bridge – I remember there was a little wooden shop where the petrol station is now. I felt safe and happy to wander.

You could identify that people didn't have the things that we had in England, but at that age it was an adventure – everyone sleeping in one room; the kitchen being in a separate block, the chickens running around the yard, the pigs, mango trees. There was a lot to

221

take in; everything was constant learning and re-education – and amazing, watching the women washing in the river. It was wow! It was deep, very deep.

In England, you're there but certain elements don't make you feel that you belong. Here, everyone raised you, embraced you; everyone in the village had time for you and received you warmly. It was all smiles, no aggression, a lot of love, and it had a massive impact on how I felt about the region, and how I felt about being in the UK, even at that young age. That experience had positives and negatives. A negative was that I felt I didn't belong in England so why was I there, so I sort of rejected the UK, but the positive was that I had a sense of belonging for the first time in my life; I didn't feel that I was part of the lost generation. For the first time I had roots. From then on, I had an affiliation with Dominica and always knew I would come back. I always maintained an interest in what was going on here, talking to my mum about relatives I met when I was a little boy. But I didn't know when I'd come back, perhaps as a pensioner, a retiree myself, but then things changed.

My parents were raised in Dominica and sent for as teenagers by their parents who were already in England. I was born in Hillingdon Hospital in west London, and we lived in Greater London in Hayes, Middlesex. It was tough: there was extreme racism and I tried to make considerable efforts to fit into a community that was different to the one our parents were from. Our parents raised us in Dominican fashion in a household where you support what your parents support, and every reference in what they were teaching us or telling us was a reference back to here. You always felt a sense of belonging to Dominica even though you hadn't been there. So we were always different to other children irrespective of ethnicity. Although there wasn't many ethnic people where we lived, we were close to a community of Dominicans in Southall. Most of those people, like my parents, were from Salisbury so we were always around our grandparents and our extended family on both sides so that was a very strong bond.

My father's death completely changed me in my outlook. Nothing's permanent, we always postpone things and opportunities are wasted. My parents always had a passion for Dominica – when my Dad spoke about Dominica, you could see his body change – his eyes lit up. His determination to return here was unbelievable. As a boy in Dominica he was seen as a bit of a naughty boy – the teachers wouldn't teach him – so he was seen as a bit of a a toe-rag. He went to England with that on his shoulder: he had a quest to prove everybody wrong – to work hard, make a success of himself and come back and show everybody what he had achieved. He was ill in hospital but still pursuing his quest to come here. He said, "It's my dream, even if I only spend one night in Dominica before I die, I'm going to do it" – but he passed away about six weeks before he was due to travel. For his funeral, we draped his coffin with a Dominican flag from the High Commission, and we got a Dominican flag to put in his hand: we thought it was fitting he was buried with part of Dominica close to him..

That was in 2001: I had booked to come down with a group of cousins and my father, by pure coincidence, had booked on the same flight. That would have been the first time that I would have been here with him. But I still came and, because I look like my dad, I would be walking up and down the village and they would say, "He's gone, but he's not gone." It was strange. We spent most of the time in the village – dominoes, the rum shop. It was crazy. There were so many of us and we're a lively bunch. That trip is legendary. People still mention it.

I was working at that time as a senior software engineer project managing and designing software. Although I had come out of school with zero qualifications, I am a first-class honours graduate and worked in the corporate world for some big international companies. Soon after that visit to Dominica, I got made redundant. It was funny, a group of us said that the redundancy was ethnic cleansing – there weren't many black people in the company anyway but 50% of the black people got made redundant – that was our internal joke, but whether it's going to tribunals, getting pay offs and so on there are a lot of problems for young ethnic professionals in the workplace in the UK.

After I was made redundant in May 2001, my gran, my mum's mum, passed away. I came down that time on my own but I was embraced really warmly and got closer to the community. I was helping organising the funeral – I'd never experienced a Caribbean funeral before and so I was watching the community come together to bury one of their own. I said to my mum, "What are you going to do for wreaths? There's no Interflora." My mum said, "That'll be taken care of", and then in the morning I saw the women, sitting on their upturned pails, making the wreaths and weaving the flowers in. And my mum got a goat slaughtered. The whole thing was really personal – walking through the village and seeing activities connected to the funeral. You see the community in action. Everyone was involved – that closeness again. You are amongst people you are at one with.

That was when it started to trigger – that second trip – it made me think there's something special here; you can't explain it but there's something special here. And I came back again in February 2003 – I was on a roll – this time with my wife who's of Jamaican descent. I said to her, "Come and see what it's like in Dominica because one day I'd like to settle here." By that time I got classified as someone who takes Dominica seriously rather than just as a passing tourist, and they treated me completely differently. We had got married earlier, and everyone knew about the wedding; one of my cousins was out here on holiday and he said, "You two are like the Posh and Becks of Salisbury. Everyone keeps going on about it." That was good banter. They treated us so well. My wife was so impressed about how people interacted with us and with her.

I had got another job in 2001 and kept coming down on visits. But after an episode at work I knew I wanted out of the corporate environment. I decided every job I took from then on was just to plan my way to Dominica. Then one day in 2004, my best friend John who I have known since I was 13, an English guy – we sat next to each other in school – said to me, "I'm leaving. I'm going to Dominica. You keep going on about it so much, if it's so great, why can't I go?" He'd never been to Dominica so we decided to go for two weeks in January 2005 to see how he would get on. I thought the Salisbury village would be too hard-core for him so we stayed in Mero. Even though he knows my family, the real deal is far more intense.

One thing I find on each trip is that once you qualify, you're OK, but then the next person has to go through the same process. And because John was white, the colonial past and stuff, it was a little harder. I think there's a bit of racism ingrained in the culture – when some people see him they think he's got loads of money and he's come here to take advantage so we'll try to empty out his wallet as quickly as possible and give him nothing in return. So I was trying to protect him from that. But at the same time to show him that if you're cool with people here, they're generally cool with you and that you need to stand firm.

So in 2006 we took a leap of faith. We didn't really have a plan – nothing firm but we did have some strong business concepts. The primary business that we came to do was the construction stuff. There's a deeper, ethical aspect to that – it's basically the story about my dad leaving me some real estate, and then getting it managed and getting ripped off. I knew all those returnees' horror stories, so when I'm here I'll always look at how things are done. When I was a bricklayer for six years, before I was a graduate, I always worked for companies who bought land and built homes of standard. I'm accustomed to be more high end. So I looked at what was going on here and thought this isn't right.

For me there's also another aspect: so many people left and went to England, all the children are born and educated in England, and have all the skills but no one brings anything back. Returnees come back, with money, but they're retired and you can't expect them to invest into concepts here because a lot of them don't understand business enough and because they're being ripped off anyway they're reluctant. So I thought, something's got to give here. I've got knowledge from overseas, I have relations with returnees and also with their children and within those relationships there must be a way of unlocking business potential. I had a business idea, and so John and I had a lot of in depth discussions as to how we could make it work here.

What we're putting together is a construction and project management company – it's called First Island Estates – primarily to manage builds on behalf of overseas clients. The core focus is the returnees. My personal ethical aspect is to be able to help repatriate some old lady who's sitting in some dingy place in east London, dying to get out and thinking she'd love to go home but "I afraid of giving builders money and they run off with it." Even if I could bring one old lady back I'd be the happiest man on the planet.

West Central restaurant in Salisbury, which we opened in

November 2007, was never in the equation, but we needed a project to start a portfolio and as a contingency.

My dad's greatest dream was to spend one night in his house in Dominica but it didn't happen. I'm sure if someone had said, "Would you sacrifice your pension to spend one night in Dominica?" he would have done it. Sometimes you have to evaluate what things stand for – quality of life has gone up to the top of the list of priorities. We have readjusted our lives in order to attain that – as opposed to a good job, a good salary. Sometimes I have a chuckle: you wouldn't get out of bed in England for the monthly gross takings here. But I can exonerate myself from that because I have come for the quality of life.

I just took my chances to come back but I still have property in England – that was a condition to coming here: my wife wanted to keep a home in the UK, and see how it goes. A lot of my friends back in England described me as "brave", some relatives thought I was crazy – but if you knew what I knew you wouldn't be saying that. It was an informed decision – I've been coming here for years and every time I see it with different eyes. I look at the business opportunities; but it's not just in Dominica, it's looking at business opportunities across the region.

I still have a lot to learn about Dominica, about my roots and family history, and in order to achieve those things I felt I had to be in Salisbury. Also here's the security issue: yes, we know that Dominica's a safe country but if you go to a village you're not from, you have more issues. You've got all that uphill stuff to go through. In Salisbury, once people can identify you back to senior relatives, the same privileges fall unto me. From the academic point of view, my children are being taught by family members – the head of the primary school is a family member and other teachers are family members. I know the level of interaction we can have with the teachers – you can't buy that.

But it's hard here. It's a heavy adjustment and the country's going through difficult times but that's happening everywhere anyway. The biggest frustration is it takes too long to do things from a business point of view, and the lack of professionalism. When you work alongside some people here, they don't understand the vision, the breadth of thought, and sometimes it's frustrating to get yourself across. People say, "We do it like this and that's how we're going to do it." Then you say, "I can show you a way that's quicker and easier for everyone." But no. There's a heavy resistance to change and there's very poor change management and those two things will dictate the future of Dominica. I want Dominica to succeed, not for my own financial benefit but for the benefit of the island – I want to be part of something that's growing, and to be proud to say I'm Dominican and that is what it means.

If people come back with the right attitudes and stamp their feet a little, things will change. Or if business A does things a certain way and business B does things a certain way, people who come back will gravitate to the business that's more professional and maybe the other business will raise its game a little. Even customer service is unbelievably bad. It doesn't bother me, in a sense, if someone is rude; I can crack a joke and defuse it, but for someone like John, I feel embarrassed because John is a genuine investor who could have gone anywhere else in the world. Dominicans are intelligent but sometimes people let themselves down by not displaying their intelligence. I've had discussions with other people in my age group who have come back, and there's a big plantocracy issue here. I've said to people, "You need to emancipate yourself from mental slavery." Maybe I might be out of place to say it but that's what I saw.

> ❛ There's a heavy resistance to change and there's very poor change management and those two things will dictate the future of Dominica. I want Dominica to succeed, not for my own financial benefit but for the benefit of the island – I want to be part of something that's growing, and to be proud to say I'm Dominican. ❜

I've had discussions with my staff and I've said to them, "When you're working for me you're actually working for yourself and if you work hard for yourself you will bear the fruit of that." I say to them that every person you serve in West Central is a future employer or a friend of a future employer. That's the attitude that should be adopted and not, "I just want my money." If I can give someone else a positive nudge, I try to do that. I think that with the team I'm working with currently some things seem to have filtered through. I like to think there's been a change. I honestly believe we are at a point in time where there are opportunities to do very, very well in Dominica, and Dominica can do very, very well as a result of it.

Dominicans, who haven't travelled, don't understand how hard it was in England, they think it was easy and we're loaded, but it has to be said that some returnees cause the problem as well – they show off. Some of the friction is from some of the returnees displaying the wrong attitude to people who have never left and some is the jealousy of people who build big houses and so on. This whole overcharging thing, it's wrong, and I've been a victim of it. But above this you never hear on the television or radio that there is a conscious effort to unite Dominicans internationally. But with West

Central I've got to meet a lot of Dominicans who are not from my village. People pull in and say, "Who owns this? Is it Dominican?" Then they think, this guy's alright. I want it to be for everybody – to sit down together, eat food and listen to music.

I have been received well here, and one of the ministers said, "How did you come up with the idea of First Island Estates? It's fantastic." And I said to him, "It came from the heart. I wanted to do something positive to help." You see the people who came back here, they raised me – the influence they've had on my life is massive; if it wasn't for that generation I would have no kinship to here. I feel indebted to that generation so when people criticise them or treat them badly I take it quite personally. In my eyes, I believe every returnee who comes back is almost like a returning war hero – Dominicans should be embracing them. For every Dominican who goes to study now in the States or in England, if it wasn't for the blows that people took or gave, they would not be going to study.

The worst thing for me here I think is the attitude towards this English thing – I don't like it. As far as I'm concerned I'm Dominican. Our house in London was a Dominican house. I've always felt a part of Dominica; I've never felt I was English. The way that people are received when they come, it's quite sad. After all, the people who are leaving today are tomorrow's returnees, and when they come back they are going to be treated like us.

Perhaps it's worse for the Dominicans who went to England because of the colonial master experience – it wasn't like that for Dominicans who went to north America. So there's got to be more of a resentment towards the Brits. Plus there's the currency – the people who come from England, they spend money – and it's noted. Whereas people from the US, don't spend that sort of money, and not so many people return here either. There's more jealousy towards the English – "another big house of the Englishman" – there's always that.

I think there's a lack of understanding on how deep these issues are and we need to eradicate that "them" and "us" concept and accept that we are one people, geographically spread who have the same goal at heart, or love at heart for that one small island. So if I can contribute even something small to making people see things that way, then I will do it.

I want my children to grow up in Dominica. My son is at the local pre-school – he was student of the year. I saw his folder, and he's flying. The children are ahead of the UK already. That's massive. The kids here are raised to focus on academic success. A child who does well at school is respected, he's cool, whereas in England the one with the latest i-pod or Nike trainer is cool. The ethnic thing is also a big thing – when I was going to school in England even though you are told you can achieve anything, the reality is that through the media you rarely see that achievement. Whereas in Dominica, you put the telly on and you see every profession there is. Everyone is just like my children or just like me. Now psychologically, I don't know how you can measure the impact of that; I would have loved to have seen that, but for my children it will be the norm. In England, it dismantles the self-esteem of the black child, and as a parent the amount of effort you have to spend in trying to counteract that. You shouldn't have to do that but you do and that takes a lot out of you itself. Cousins who were educated here have gone out in the world and there's nothing that they can't achieve, and that's what I want my kids to have. I'm learning patois and my children will learn that too – they will have a full cultural experience.

I'm trying to encourage people all the time to come back home. When I blow the trumpet, I tell them, pack your things; it's as simple as that. My motive is this: Dominica needs investment and there's no better an investor than a son of the soil, and I will try to draw as many of those people here as I possibly can.

At the end of the day, the battles here are nothing compared to the battles on the other side. Even if I've said negative things and that things are tough here, it's only frustrations not stress. And at the end of the day, if you take a sea bath or sit on the veranda, sip on a juice and watch the sea, those things dissolve. You don't carry it from one day to the next, whereas in the UK you carry it, and it gets heavier by the day. ■